MODELING
CITIES & TOWNS

Jeff Wilson

Kalmbach
Media

On the cover: New York Central's elevated West Side freight line was designed to ease congestion on busy city streets. It's now an urban park. *New York Central*

On the back cover: An Illinois Terminal interurban leads a short freight through Bloomington, Ill. (left) *Henry J. McCord;* A Burlington freight heads down Main Street, built of Walthers modular street sections, on a scene built by Jeff Wilson. *Jeff Wilson*

Kalmbach Media
21027 Crossroads Circle
Waukesha, Wisconsin 53186
www.KalmbachHobbyStore.com

© 2020 Kalmbach Media

Published in 2020
24 23 22 21 20   1 2 3 4 5

Manufactured in China

ISBN: 978-1-62700-759-7
EISBN: 978-1-62700-760-3

Editor: Eric White
Book Design: Lisa Schroeder

Library of Congress Control Number: 2019948815

Contents

A Kansas City Southern E8 departs Texarkana, Texas, in July 1952. Urban modeling offers many varied appealing facets, such as the multi-track passenger terminal, complex trackwork, and wide variety of industrial buildings with lots of freight and passenger cars to be switched. *R.S. Plummer; Louis A. Marre collection*

Introduction

The late Earl Smallshaw, a master of creating realistic city scenes (see **3-11**), said urban scenes will always draw the most attention from visitors on a model railroad, and I agree with him. Towns and cities offer the largest potential for a high level of detailing in a relatively small space, with vehicles, figures, signs, streets, and structures—plus the trains themselves.

A well-done city scene can hold a viewer's attention for hours as they try to find all of the scenes-within-scenes and hidden details. Cities offer a multitude of opportunities for mini-scenes and extensive details—modelers can keep adding details long after the basic area or layout is "finished."

City modeling has a lot to offer. You can build a relatively small (let's say 2 x 8-foot) layout, but include enough structures and associated details to remain busy for many years of modeling. You can also add a city extension to an existing layout, or turn an existing scene into a city industrial area or edge of a town—and it won't take a lot of room to do so.

The flip side is modeling urban areas can take a lot of time, effort, and modeling resources. It's good to learn some tricks for focusing your talents and the best use of your available time to complete it.

City train operations don't give you long stretches of fast running with long trains, but operations in industrial areas, passenger terminals, and similar areas are slower paced—often reflecting actual time when switching compared to the prototype. A relatively small area of complex trackwork with multiple spurs and customers can keep operators busy for hours.

You can model freight operations, passenger operations and terminals, or both. Large passenger terminals were focal points of many major cities, and provide a chance to model passenger trains of multiple railroads by modeling a union station and its related yards and trackwork.

Challenges

Modeling a town, city, or urban area in a realistic manner involves a lot more than plopping down some large groups of structures along the tracks. Because cities are so large (and the buildings are often quite tall), it's almost impossible to model them to scale. This means capturing the feel while shrinking the models, an art known as "selective compression." An example might be taking a prototype passenger station with 12 through tracks and building it in the same style, but shorter and with just 6 tracks. This keeps the flavor and essence of the real thing, but allows it to better fit on a layout. Another trick is to model the largest buildings and key structures as photos on the backdrop or as building flats.

Even with smaller towns, it's impossible to model them completely to scale on an average layout. That's when selective compression again comes in, perhaps by omitting buildings that don't contribute operationally to the railroad, and by concentrating on structures and features that capture the flavor of a town.

You can have well-built, beautifully detailed, realistic buildings and other models, but a scene will fall apart realistically if the arrangement is not done in a realistic manner or if details from contrasting eras are featured. Signs, vehicles, structure styles, and details like traffic lights and street markings must fit in with the period you're modeling if you want a scene to have the proper "feel" and mood.

Chapter 1 opens with a look at how prototype cities and towns were designed, the different ways they were laid out, how they evolved, and how railroads prompted this evolution. The following chapters examine the various elements of cities and towns. We'll see how structures assume much of the role of scenery in urban areas, and look at items such as retaining walls, streets, sidewalks, signs, bridges, and the railroad right-of-way fit in. Along the way we'll examine methods of effectively modeling various town and urban features, maximizing operating potential while saving space by using building flats and other details.

Horseback riders known as West Side Cowboys preceded New York Central trains along 10th Avenue in New York City. The vehicles, signs, locomotive, railcars, brick streets, and other details place this scene in a specific time—you could probably make a good guess about the period even if you didn't know the photo was taken in 1941. *New York Central*

CHAPTER ONE

City and town design and evolution

A Milwaukee Road switcher works in Minneapolis near the passenger depot, with the city's distinctive and extensive flour milling district in the background. Industrial areas dominated cities along railroad tracks through the 1940s. The wood walkways are a sharp detail.
Henry J. McCord

The key to realistically modeling large urban areas and towns is to use prototype examples as guides, and to understand how towns and railroads grew around each other and what real railroads and city planners needed and wanted. Capturing large cities can be a challenge due to our limited modeling spaces, and in any town or city it's important to focus on the elements that best reflect the flavor of a locale or region, **1**.

Cities and towns are "compactly settled areas," says Webster's, of varying sizes, but it can be difficult to precisely define the difference between a town and a city—or between a "small city" and "large city." Most literal definitions center on the type of government as opposed to size or other physical features, which doesn't really matter to modelers. Far more important to us are the importance of railroads in the area, the types and sizes of structures, the industries, and the streets and other details—the elements that give a town or urban area a specific feeling.

To me, for modeling purposes a town is a settled area that's large enough to have a railroad depot (or to have had one in the steam and early diesel eras). The presence of a depot likely meant a place large enough to also rate one or more rail-served businesses or industries, and thus worthy of capturing on a model railroad.

Smaller villages (or sometimes simply groups of dwellings, perhaps with a store and/or gas station) that railroads didn't deem worthy of a depot, likely won't have rail-served businesses and won't be divided by streets into blocks of residences or businesses.

Cities imply large metropolitan centers, characterized by a large downtown business district, multiple areas of retail businesses and neighborhoods, high-rise buildings, public transportation systems, a large railroad terminal, and multiple large industries and rail lines.

We'll keep our discussions focused on towns and cities that are served by railroads, and look at how railroads influenced city design and characteristics—and vice versa. Let's start with a look at towns, then move up to cities and large urban areas.

Towns
Characteristics of a town include a central area with storefront buildings, a gathering of houses, and several small industries or businesses (grain elevator, fuel dealer, etc.) served by rail, **2**. The town is divided into blocks, with a main highway or two passing through. These main roads may or may not be the town's "main street."

Lines of Illinois Central, Baltimore & Ohio, and Chicago & Eastern Illinois cross at the western edge of Tuscola, Ill., in 1984. Central Street East and West parallel the B&O and C&EI tracks with storefront buildings on each street in a typical Midwestern scene. *Gordon E. Lloyd*

Rock Island's double-track main line through Sheffield, Ill, is well-maintained in this 1940s scene, while the spur tracks serving the elevator and other businesses are weedy. The depot is a focal point; note the house track behind it, along with the water towers and water fill spouts—vital for steam locomotives. *Ira H. Eigsti*

The rail line may have a passing siding and one or more spurs to serve the local industries, **3**. There may be a second railroad passing through town, with a grade crossing in or next to the town.

Structures in towns are generally modest in size. A small town may still have one- and two-story wood-frame structures along its main streets well into the diesel era, and might not have uniform sidewalks or curbs and gutters along the streets. Dirt streets and roads were also common in some regions (especially in the West and plains states) into the 1940s.

Larger towns began to feature a lot of brick construction by the early 1900s,

with buildings abutting each other. These could be a single story, but two- to four-story structures were common. Streets in larger towns were usually paved by the early 1900s, with concrete sidewalks as well as curbs and gutters.

The bigger the town, the larger the business district—it may stretch several blocks and perhaps extend to multiple cross streets, **4**. Larger towns will have more (and larger) businesses and industries, which means more rail spurs and sidings. These industries may be located in a separate area of the town. Another characteristic of larger towns is a downtown park or square, perhaps adjoining a courthouse or near the railroad station.

The population of Sayre, Pa., peaked around 8,000, but it was an important point on the Lehigh Valley. It had a substantial station, yard (crossed by pedestrian and street bridges), and several blocks of businesses. *Jack Boucher, Historic American Engineering Record*

Depots will be signature elements of almost any small town model scene into the 1960s. Details at Winchester, Ill., on the Burlington in 1954 include the platform, surrounding track, signs, train-order board, sidewalk, crossing, communication pole, and crossing flashers. *Henry J. McCord*

Depots were important locations through the 1950s, **5**. They were important for serving passengers, receiving and shipping less-than-carload (LCL) merchandise and express, and for being the communication point between dispatchers and train crews (especially along railroads controlled by timetable and train order operations). The depot will often be central to the town; usually adjacent to a main street, often with a team track around the rear of the station.

Larger towns usually meant larger railroad stations, with passenger trains more likely to stop, and possibly a separate freight station. The familiar green trucks of the Railway Express Agency were common, even in small towns.

As passenger train service and LCL traffic declined and railroads moved toward radio communication, depots began closing in large numbers by the 1960s (especially in smaller communities).

6

Martin, Ky., is a small coal mining town on the Chesapeake & Ohio (population 1,100 in 1950). It boasted a substantial station (center), small coal-marshaling yard (far left), wye leading to a branch, and several curving streets tucked between the hills, creek, and railroad. *Trains magazine collection*

Town design

What each of us thinks of as a "typical" town varies greatly depending upon the region and era. The basic layout of a railroad town is dependent upon several things: geography (rivers, lakes, mountains, hills), highways and roads, prominent local industries, and when the town came into existence (and whether the town or railroad came first).

The layout of a town varies greatly by region. In the East, especially in mountainous areas, individual streets and block/grid patterns tend to follow geographic features, **6**. Many are long and narrow, following a valley along a stream or river. They may have limited side streets and/or streets that curve and angle.

In the Midwest and plains states, town blocks are more likely to follow a grid pattern, though tracks may cross at an angle, **7**. Towns may be longer or narrower, following main through roads. The grid likely aligns most streets north-south and east-west, following

the lines of country roads, which are spaced a mile apart, dividing farmland into mile-square, 640-acre "sections."

The diagrams in **8** show a few common types of town arrangements, showing several ways that railroads passed through them. Keys to realistically modeling towns include the track layout and arrangement itself, then the arrangement of buildings, streets, roads, and other features.

As you look at these—and as you look at photos and explore real locations—you'll see that railroads often pass through towns at angles that didn't match the street grid. As the drawings show, most streets kept to their grid, with some alterations made for railroad tracks. There were exceptions, however, where the main grid was angled to match the railroad (or a river). Also remember that there are few communities where all streets follow a grid: All towns and cities seem to have at least a few funky intersections and winding streets.

If a railroad was late to arrive to a town that had already been established, the tracks usually skirt the edge of town. The depot would likely be near wherever the town's main street crosses the tracks. Later businesses (grain elevators, oil companies, etc.) would eventually build along the tracks, but again on the outskirts of town.

This can create the "right/wrong side of the tracks" scenario for larger towns, as the original older part of town is on one side, while new construction develops on the other side after the railroad is established—especially if a town experienced rapid growth in the years after World War II.

Multi-railroad towns come in many variations as well. You can often tell which railroad arrived first: One may go through the heart of the town while the other skirts the edge, with the two crossing at grade (or grade-separated with a bridge) on the town's outskirts. Or perhaps one is a main line and the other is a branch or secondary line.

Tracks often cut through towns at cities at angles, as in this 1954 scene on the Chicago & North Western at DeKalb, Ill. A crossing guard holds a stop sign at left; there's also a signal in the middle of the street just to the right of the F unit's nose. *H.M. Stange; Krambles-Peterson collection*

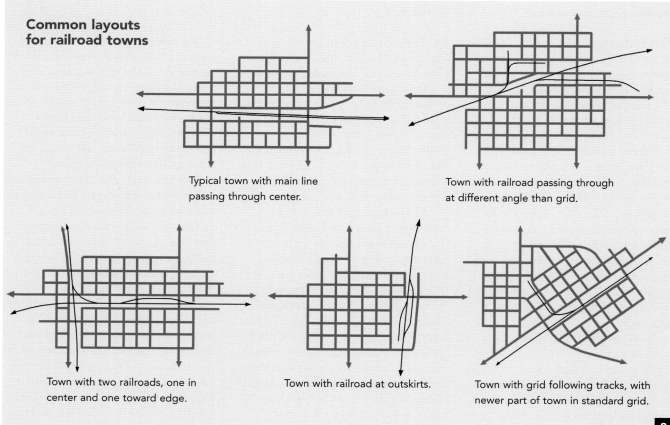

Common layouts for railroad towns

Typical town with main line passing through center.

Town with railroad passing through at different angle than grid.

Town with two railroads, one in center and one toward edge.

Town with railroad at outskirts.

Town with grid following tracks, with newer part of town in standard grid.

8

A beet train in November 1957 shows why many city and town structures look dirty and gritty in the steam era. Colorado & Southern's main line to Denver goes down the middle of Mason Street in Fort Collins, Colo. *Jim Ehrenberger*

If both railroads arrived early—common as many towns were established and then grew where rail lines crossed—they may both run through the heart of the town. A shared depot is a possibility, or separate depots located near each other.

If a railroad establishes a town, or if a town grows after the railroad has been built, the railroad likely will go through the heart of the business district (and possibly right down main street, **9**). This means the railroad figured in the formal plotting of blocks and other features.

The main street—not necessarily by name, but the street with most storefront businesses and buildings—usually follows one of two styles. It can run parallel to the railroad, **10**. If you like modeling storefront structures and downtown scenes, this arrangement will appeal to you, **11**. A downside is that this style of town can take up a lot of layout space.

The other arrangement is for the main street to cross the railroad, **12**. This is common for many small towns, and for some larger towns where the railroad skirts the edge of town. It can be great for conserving space on a layout: Especially on a shelf-style layout—an entire town can be simulated by a simple cross street running from the fascia to the backdrop, with a few buildings and perhaps a spur to a local industry.

In most towns, the number of streets crossing the tracks is minimized as much as possible. Main streets will have grade crossings, but many secondary and side streets will be truncated before the tracks. This is especially true for main lines hosting a lot of traffic at high speed. For busy lines, crossings will be protected by gates and flashers.

Branch lines and other low-traffic, low-speed lines will have more crossings, and these might be protected only by signs (crossbucks), requiring train crews to stop and "flag" the crossings as they pass through.

If the railroad has a passing siding at a town, it is often arranged so that most of it stretches into the country (perhaps with one end of it in town

Main streets in many towns run parallel to the tracks, as shown in this 1908 view of Gallup, N.M., along the Santa Fe. The buildings on the corner are still standing. Note the trees being planted along the streets. *Library of Congress*

Modeling a scene where the railroad runs parallel to the main street is great for modeling lots of storefront buildings and roadside businesses, but can take up a lot of layout space. Pelle Søeborg modeled this modern Union Pacific scene in HO. *Pelle Søeborg*

near the depot), again to minimize grade crossings—crossings are avoided on passing sidings whenever possible to avoid blocking streets and roads by stopped trains.

Towns that served as "railroad towns"—those which served as division points or crew-change points, hosted shop and engine facilities, or perhaps were the headquarters for a small railroad—may have a yard or other extensive trackage in town, **13**. As this and the photo of Sayre (**4**) show, these wouldn't have streets passing through them, but may have highway or pedestrian bridges passing over them. The depot (which may be large, even though the town is not) and other

support structures will be nearby. The view from a rail yard is generally the rear of commercial buildings along neighboring streets.

Town evolution

Town sizes fluctuated widely from the 1800s into the early 1900s. Boom and bust towns were common, especially in areas with industries such as lumber and mining. Many towns simply shrunk and died as industries (or raw-material sources) moved away—the Depression killed off many small towns as well—while others grew dramatically as new businesses came to town.

Small towns saw great changes from the 1960s onward, which should

be reflected on a model railroad, as these changes reflect eras and regions being re-created. Many towns began shrinking as small schools closed and school districts consolidated, influencing people to move to larger towns and cities.

The rural economy changed greatly. Areas that once supported hundreds of family farms saw the number and size of families shrink and the number of farms decline dramatically. By the 1960s and '70s, those who still lived in rural areas and small towns were more likely to do their shopping in larger towns.

Businesses in small rural towns were no longer supported by the shrinking rural population and changes in

shopping habits, and vacant storefronts (and entire blocks) became common. Meanwhile, in larger towns, many retail businesses moved from downtown areas to malls or to strips along the "miracle mile"—the major highways and roads approaching towns.

The types of businesses in towns changed as well. Through the 1960s, many featured independent drug stores, hardware stores, groceries, and other specialty shops such as shoe and clothing stores. Those that didn't close or move often became affiliated with chain brands, and the number of small and regional chain brands shrunk and were absorbed by larger companies.

By the turn of the 21st century, the small-town local grocery store had largely been replaced by large supermarkets and smaller mini-marts, and traditional gas station "service stations" were replaced by convenience stores and separate auto-repair businesses.

Railroads themselves were doing less business in towns. Depots began disappearing in large numbers from the 1960s through the 1970s as passenger trains disappeared and railroads moved to radio communication and track-warrant control, replacing the timetable-and-train-order systems that were dependent on depot-based local operators. Railroad-based less-than-carload (LCL) shipments, a vital part of small depots' operations through the 1940s, had all but disappeared by the late 1960s, moving to trucks.

As small depots were closed, most were simply torn down; others were preserved and kept by railroads as maintenance bases, or sold to serve as other businesses or local museums.

The number of rail-served industries in small towns and cities also began dropping by that period. Small, inefficient grain elevators, for example, closed and were replaced by larger facilities that could load large cuts of cars (or entire trains) at once.

Other "typical" local businesses largely moved to truck transportation only, including many of what we think of as traditional rail-served traffic: oil dealers, lumber yards, feed suppliers, food wholesalers—or disappeared almost completely, like coal dealers.

Keep a few general guidelines in mind when designing towns. Remember that any given photo shows just a thin slice of a town. Likewise, what we model can only capture a small slice of the real thing (even for a small town), so focus on the features that appeal to you as a modeler and that will help you with your layout's operations.

Cities

A city is not only physically larger than a town, with a higher population—it has many other characteristics as well, **14**. For railroads, this usually means extensive yards and shop facilities, and junctions and interchanges with other railroads (or points where separate divisions head in different directions). Trains (passenger as well as freight) originate and terminate in cities.

Cities will have large, tall structures: most feature an extensive central downtown area of multi-story high-rise buildings housing both offices and retail businesses, **15**. Compared to a town, streets will be wider, traffic will be heavier, there will be more people, and everything will have a busier feel to it.

Along with the downtown, most cities have extensive industrial areas—served by railroads, **1**—sprawling over many acres of real estate. The key is that unlike towns, which typically have small businesses that receive a car or two of goods, industries in cities

The main streets of some towns are perpendicular to the tracks (note the boxcar behind the line of vehicles at left). Modeling scenes this way takes up less room on a layout. This is Lake Lillian, Minn. *Jeff Wilson collection*

13

14

The Rutland Railroad had a small yard in its namesake city in Vermont. A train has just arrived at the station at far right in this 1957 view. The distant hills and the back walls of the many city structures frame the scene nicely. *Jim Shaughnessy*

A Rock Island commuter train behind an RS-3 speeds southward out of Chicago in the 1960s. City scenes will be dominated by large structures, complex trackwork, and industrial areas. *Donald Sims*

produce or process products on a huge scale, resulting in dozens or hundreds of cars of traffic on a regular basis. It's entirely possible to base an entire model railroad on a single industry or industrial area in a city, **16**.

Cities also include multiple residential areas and neighborhoods, plus substantial suburbs, which may sprawl several miles outward from the city itself. However fascinating these areas might be, for modelers, these areas are generally far away from the scenes along the tracks that we model.

A signature feature of most cities is a transportation system. Almost all had streetcars through the steam era (more on those in Chapter 7), **17**, with extensive trackage through the downtown area with lines extending to industrial districts and residential areas. The increasing popularity of the automobile spelled the end for most of these systems by the 1940s, with cities switching to bus service after that.

Many cities feature commuter trains, hosted either by railroads or a separate commuter agency. These can operate on either private rights-of-way or on lines of conventional railroads (or a combination of the two).

Tall structures, including office buildings and those with first-floor storefronts, dominate city street scenes. Pedestrian traffic is heavy in this 1943 view of Houston, Texas.
John Vachon, Library of Congress

Chuck Hitchcock's HO scale Argentine Industrial District layout is a basement-size model railroad entirely devoted to re-creating terminal, industrial, and yard switching in the Kansas City area circa 1960. *Paul J. Dolkos*

Large passenger terminals (some cities have multiple stations) are often signature structures in cities, **18**. These may be owned by a single railroad, or shared among two or more lines (union stations). Differentiating these from passenger depots in smaller towns is that at terminals, passenger trains often originated, terminated, and were serviced—they weren't just passing through. Supporting these were passenger yards, where cars were sorted, cleaned, and stored.

Their size can make them difficult to model, but some modelers have made them key components of their layouts. Chapter 6 goes into detail on terminals and related details and trackage.

City evolution and changes

Most large cities grew around railroads through the late 1800s. As industries were built and rail lines expanded to serve them, cities grew outward from this center. Most historical industrial areas in cities were near their downtowns, near ready supplies of labor. These manufacturing plants along rail lines (and sometimes waterways as well) typically featured the heavy, substantial, brick multi-story construction common to that era.

Railroads built yards in cities, along with extensive locomotive servicing facilities, car-repair shops, freight houses, warehouses, headquarters buildings, and other structures. As

cities grew, these yards and shops became hemmed in by surrounding industries, streets, and structures.

This is why railroads travel straight through the heart of most large cities, with the railroad typically in the "old" part of the city. The railroad was a huge part of the city, connecting businesses and people, and taking on the personality of the city as well.

As discussed earlier with towns, railroads avoided grade crossings as much as possible in cities, **19**. As vehicle traffic increased in the early 1900s, many railroads moved to elevate trackwork; in other areas, crossings were eliminated where possible, with streets elevated on bridges. Chapter 4 has more details.

The era after World War II saw major changes in large cities, especially regarding railroads. People were leaving city centers to move into suburbs and outlying housing developments. Industries in traditional city manufacturing centers were aging and finding it difficult to expand and rebuild in existing areas. These older plants began closing, with many moving outward to suburbs and other surrounding areas where there was more space, cheaper land, and better access to highways—including the emerging interstate highway system. Smaller industries were moving to truck transportation instead of railroads.

Railroads, which were beginning to

A pair of streetcars pass on Market Street in Louisville in the 1910s. Streetcars were signature elements of major cities through the 1930s. Note the brick street, overhead wires, and city structures and signs.
Library of Congress

build new, modern yards, also turned to outlying areas, where they were not limited by space constrictions of surrounding buildings, rivers, roads, and other obstructions. Security was also easier to control, as problems with trespassing, theft, and vandalism were increasing in urban yard areas.

As diesel locomotives took over in the 1940s and later, the extensive shop facilities required to maintain steam—almost all of which were located in cities—were no longer needed, which

Dallas Union Station was a prominent structure in that city's downtown area. This 1940s view shows several trains in the station's through tracks. The coach yard is at upper right. *Historic American Engineering Record*

As cities grew, so did both vehicle and railroad traffic as shown in this late 1920s view of New York City's west side. New York Central's 33rd Street Freight Station is at left. Elevated track, street bridges, and elimination of railroad crossings were a goal of railroads and cities alike. *New York Central*

reduced the number of railroad workers needed as well. Some of these facilities were cut down in size to serve diesels; others were eliminated and moved.

By the 1960s, passenger traffic was dropping dramatically. Terminals saw drastic reductions, and many were closed with remaining service handled at smaller stations, often away from city centers. The coming of Amtrak in 1971 saw the large-scale closing of many passenger facilities.

Related express traffic (Railway Express Agency) and railroad LCL traffic were also in steep decline, with most freight houses and large express terminals closed by 1970.

All of this, along with many other economic factors, meant many of the traditional city areas along railroad rights-of-way became run-down, with industrial areas abandoned or shrunken, buildings and terminals vacant, stores and businesses closing or diminished, and neighborhoods in these areas facing higher crime rates and other problems.

From the 1940s to the 1970s, the amount of industrial trackage in cities dropped dramatically, with many trunk lines also removed as railroads merged, consolidated traffic, and trimmed branch and secondary lines. Many areas that had been thriving and active in the 1940s were abandoned and quiet by the 1960s and '70s.

City modeling guidelines

Because of the sheer size of cities and urban areas, selective compression is necessary to capture these areas in miniature. Focus on modeling specific scenes and details, not the entire city. As Chapter 3 discusses, there are many ways to effectively capture the look and atmosphere of a large city through photo backdrops and building flats combined with foreground structures.

If you're modeling a specific prototype, study photos from the appropriate period and find scenes that appeal to you. You also know what is most important to you as a modeler: Is it operation? Building structures? Re-creating realistic scenes?

Keep structures and scenes true to the eras being modeled. Study what was common for signs, company names, and business types for the period. Weathering is important to capture these effects.

Chapter 2 examines the streets themselves in great detail, and Chapter 3 shows how to capture the look and feel of cities and towns with various modeling tips and techniques.

1

CHAPTER TWO

City streets and street trackage

When modeling cities and towns, it's difficult to understate the importance of realistic streets and roads, **1**. Color, texture, and details are important, along with the street plan itself. In addition, tracks in streets were extremely common through the mid-1900s and can still be found, and these can be the focal point of a modeled scene, **2**.

An Illinois Terminal interurban leads a short freight train around a corner on a brick street in Bloomington, Ill., in 1946. Street modeling is critical for capturing the appearance of city and town scenes. *Henry J. McCord*

This HO city scene uses Walthers street track inserts with the company's street panels. *Jim Forbes*

Dirt streets were common through the 1890s, and streetcars sometimes ran on dirt streets as here on Central Avenue in Hot Springs, Ark., around 1900.
Library of Congress

Typical street cross section

Sidewalk slopes slightly toward curb

Street crowned 4"-6" in middle

Curb and gutter, 24" wide; Curb typically 6" tall; gutter typically 18" wide

Street width varies greatly

Street surface can be asphalt, concrete, or brick

Choosing the appropriate street material, coloring and weathering it realistically, and blending it with surrounding structures and scenery will help you capture the feel of the region, era, or specific prototype that you're modeling.

Dirt and gravel were the most common road and street surfaces through the 1800s, **3**, but cities and towns were commonly paving their streets by the 1900s. Dirt—the natural earth surface, even when graded and compacted—became mud with rain (or spring melting), and in extreme cases could become a quagmire impassible for both wagons and foot traffic alike. Add a healthy dose of horse manure, and you can understand why a muddy city street was not a pleasant place to trod in the 1800s.

Gravel—a mix of crushed stone and other fine aggregates—was a step better. Compacted gravel atop a crowned, compacted base allows drainage and is cleaner than dirt. Gravel surfaces became popular for rural roads, and still can be found in many areas. However, gravel was still a far-from-ideal surface for urban areas that saw heavy traffic.

It was inevitable that paved surfaces would soon become popular, especially in larger cities. Paved roads eliminated the headaches of mud, dust, and grime, and provided a smoother path for horse-drawn wagons and pedestrians. Several materials were used for paving streets, including stone, brick, concrete, and asphalt.

Cobblestones have for centuries been regarded as a preferred paving material. These rounded, natural stones (usually from rivers, where water had worn their surfaces smooth) were strong, but for the sheer volume needed, cities turned to man-made brick by the late 1800s. Bricks, which were first used to pave a street in the U.S. in 1873 (in Charleston, W.Va.) are still often called cobblestones. The first asphalt-paved street in the U.S. appeared in the 1870s and concrete was first used in Bellefontaine, Ohio, in 1891.

By the time automobiles and trucks began appearing in large numbers, major cities were paving most streets; even smaller cities and towns were at least hard-topping their main streets. Gravel streets, however, remained common in some smaller towns and even larger cities, particularly in the West, through the mid-1900s.

Street design

With any paved surface in a city, drainage becomes very important. Water from rain and melting snow needs a place to go, or flooding will result. For this reason, roads are "crowned," meaning they are higher in the middle than on the sides. This keeps water from pooling on the surface, forcing it to drain toward either side. The amount of crown varies, but 4 to 6 inches is common, and it is sometimes taller (especially on wide streets). See **4** for drawing of a typical street cross-section.

On a rural road, this runoff drains to the shoulder, where it goes to gravel, grass, or a roadside ditch. In a town or city, with its sidewalks and buildings instead of ditches, water needs a place to escape. The gutter is the lowest point along the street next to the curb, which steps up to the sidewalk or a neighboring grass surface. Water runs along the gutter, eventually reaching drains, where it flows to an underground sewer, which takes it out of sight.

Workers lay bricks on Ohio Route 40 in the summer of 1938. Paving bricks are fired differently than building bricks. *Ben Shahn, Library of Congress*

Test-fit the Walthers street panels (or other street material) with the structures you intend to use. *Jeff Wilson*

Street width varies greatly, depending upon the era it was built (or rebuilt), the space available, the amount of traffic, and the presence of parking lanes on one or both sides. Streets in many Eastern towns and cities (and in many older neighborhoods) can be quite narrow.

Meanwhile, in many areas of the West, where prairies stretched for miles and space wasn't at a premium, streets can be quite wide—up to 150 feet in some cases, with diagonal parking on each side. These wide streets fell out of favor for many reasons, mainly that they proved quite hazardous for pedestrians and cross traffic to get across. They also

required more drainage and were more expensive to maintain.

In general, main thoroughfares tend to be wider and built to higher standards, while side streets tend to be narrower. Typical lane width was 10 feet through the early 1900s, but grew to 11 and then 12 feet.

We want to convey the feel of real streets when modeling, but it's usually best to selectively compress street width to save real estate that's better used for structures and railroad right of way. As an example, a prototype two-lane street with diagonal parking will be about 52 feet wide (two 12-foot traffic lanes and two 14-foot parking

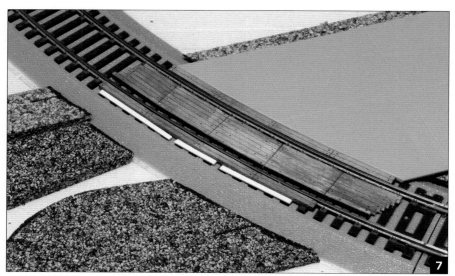

This HO wood crossing is from Blair Line. The grade crossing should extend slightly beyond the width of the road. Shims (styrene strips) raise the crossing to just below rail-top level. *Jeff Wilson*

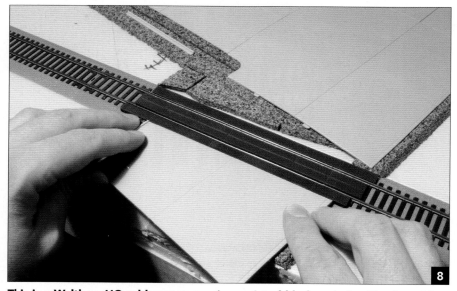

This is a Walthers HO rubber-mat crossing, painted black and glued in place. The street material can be cut for crossings that aren't square to the street. *Jeff Wilson*

strips). A pair of 10-foot traffic lanes with two 8-foot parking lanes cuts that to 36 feet (about 5" in HO). For side streets, you can eliminate parking on one side and/or make streets with a single one-way traffic lane, getting streets down to 20 feet wide while still looking realistic.

Some streets have center islands or grass areas (boulevards). These islands are sometimes shaped to guide traffic, with turn lanes. There are too many variations to list—again, follow prototype examples whenever possible.

Intersections are key interest areas. They must allow enough room for turning vehicles—a corner curb radius of about 10 feet is minimum for minor streets, with up to 18 feet for two major streets meeting to allow for semis and other long vehicles to turn.

Bike lanes have become popular in many cities in the 2000s—usually 5 or 6 feet wide, located between traffic and parking lanes. You'll also find turning lanes in most towns and metro areas. Use the prototype as a guide in designing your modeled streets.

Most city streets with street-front structures are straight, sometimes angling at intersections. Some streets will curve if needed—these are more common in urban areas where hills, mountains, rivers, and other features get in the way of street grids.

Sidewalks are a prominent part of any city scene. In urban areas where buildings are placed along streets, sidewalks are usually at least 6 feet wide, and 10 or 12 feet is common—especially where lampposts, signs, and other obstructions line the street. They may appear level, but sidewalks are designed to slope slightly toward the gutter.

Curbs provide a definitive edge to the road. A combined curb and gutter of poured concrete is standard, even if the roadway is a different surface. Most curbs are 6" tall and 6" wide, rounded at the top corner, with an 18" gutter, although many older curbs are taller.

Curb ramps (or curb cuts) at intersections first appeared in the 1940s, became common in the 1950s, and are now mandated. Early ones were simply ramps over the gutter to help people's shoes stay dry (see photo **27** in Chapter 5); today, most have curbs that drop down to the gutter level.

Another option is a "green belt" between the curb and sidewalk. This is a strip generally 3 to 6 feet wide, with grass and (sometimes) trees. These are more common in residential areas, but can be found in downtown areas as well.

Alleys run behind structures in most downtown blocks, allowing access for deliveries, private parking, and garbage pickup. Widths vary greatly, with some as narrow as 12 feet and increasing to 20 feet or more. Unlike streets, alleys generally are not crowned—instead they have a depression in the middle to allow drainage to centered grates or to neighboring street gutters.

Paving materials

Bricks were a common early paving material, **1**. They were long lasting: You can still find brick streets in use that were laid more than 100 years ago. Although they worked well in horse-and-wagon days, their rough texture and many seams made them noisy and

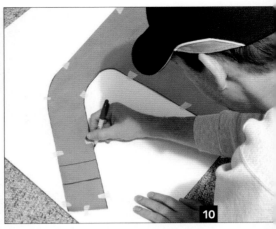

Styrene sheet works well for large areas and curved streets. The paper template makes it easy to test-fit buildings and define the exact dimensions and shape of the street. *Jeff Wilson*

Cut the paper template to shape, tape it to a large sheet of styrene, trace the outline on the styrene, and score the styrene with a hobby knife. The styrene can be snapped at the scored lines. *Jeff Wilson*

rough riding as autos became popular, with vehicles often limited to slow speeds.

Paving bricks differ from common building bricks in that paving bricks are vitrified—glazed and kilned at extremely high temperatures. This makes them more durable, less likely to crack, and impervious to moisture and chemical corrosion.

The underlying roadbed base is important for paving bricks, with a layer of gravel covered with sand, then the bricks at the top, **5**. This allows drainage and resistance to frost/freeze damage, and the many gaps allow the bricks to flex enough under load to keep the road resilient to damage.

How paving bricks are put down creates a distinctive appearance—and also makes them challenging to model realistically. Many patterns are used. Many streets have parallel rows with alternating joints, much like a building wall. Scalloped patterns (alternating at 90-degree angles) are also common, and curved patterns can also be found, especially at intersections. Rows of bricks next to gutters, at intersections, and along tracks embedded in the street often followed a different pattern compared to the rest of the street.

Visually, brick streets are compelling because they're not quite uniform—over years and decades of vehicle traffic, freeze/thaw cycles, and general

weathering and wear, individual bricks shift slightly in position and alignment. Most model offerings (and commercial brick sheet material) are simply too uniform and perfect to capture the true appearance.

Bricks are also often used for pedestrian areas, namely railroad station platforms and surrounding pathways, as well as sidewalks. Most paving bricks are dark red, and exposure to weather along with decades of oil, dirt, grime, and exhaust make them even darker.

Natural asphalt—a mix of various aggregates such as sand and limestone with bitumen (a tarry, viscous material)—has been used for paving for hundreds of years. It was first used as a paving material in the U.S. in the 1870s. Its use increased rapidly in the early 1900s with the growth of the petroleum industry, with bitumen produced as a byproduct of refining.

One of asphalt's biggest advantages is that it can be spread to suit any street configuration or shape. It was originally applied by manually spreading it, then compacting it. By the early 1900s, mixers and mechanized spreaders were doing much of the work. It was often used for patching and paving over existing brick and cobblestone streets.

The material can withstand heavy traffic, but can heave and crack (especially in areas where the ground

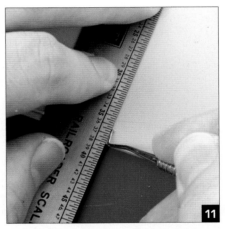

A dental pick works well for scoring lines in styrene sheet. You can also use a hobby knife flipped over and drawn backward. *Jeff Wilson*

freezes), so it requires periodic patching and repair—which alters its appearance. The average lifespan for an asphalt street is 20 to 30 years before resurfacing, so in modeling we can simulate how old a street is supposed to be by its color, patches, and repairs.

Although asphalt is close to black when initially applied, it quickly changes to progressively lighter shades of gray. A challenge in capturing this effect on model surfaces is that asphalt isn't a uniform color: It's a blend of many colors, based on the colors of the millions of individual small rocks and pebbles in the aggregates used in the mix. Depending on the local supply

The resulting styrene road and street is glued in place on the layout base (foam in this case) with water-based contact cement or latex construction adhesive.
Jeff Wilson

Plaster works well for many types of roads and streets. Mix the plaster to a thick consistency and work it into the forms, as Pelle Søeborg is doing here.
Pelle Søeborg

of aggregates, these colors can range from tan and various shades of gray to red and brown. Keep an eye for color photos of the specific area being modeled.

Concrete became popular for paving by the early 1900s. A mix of cement, sand, and gravel, concrete is harder than asphalt and was adopted for its strength and permanence, especially for city streets.

Because it isn't flexible like asphalt, concrete was poured in distinctive "panels" separated by expansion gaps, which were filled by hard rubber or similar material. This allowed for the material's expansion and contraction in heat and cold, along with movement from spring frost heaves and any settling of the subroadbed.

Modern materials and installation methods now allow concrete to be paved in continuous sheets, but there are still many older streets where the panels and expansion joints are apparent in various states of repair.

As with asphalt, concrete roadways vary widely in color. New roads are very light gray (often almost white), but they gradually weather to darker shades of grayish tan, revealing the color provided by individual pieces of aggregate and other impurities as with asphalt.

Pavement markings

Striping and other highway markings have evolved considerably since the early 1900s. Most early paved streets and roads had no markings, and sign use was very inconsistent. Individual cities and towns gradually began adding pavement striping, markings, and control signs, but they were not uniform—the style, placement, and design varied widely from area to area.

The 1910s saw the first pavement markings, with center lines first appearing in 1911 in Michigan—but the first stop sign didn't appear until 1914. As vehicle traffic increased, a move toward uniform signs and markings began. Several states adopted uniform standards by the early 1920s, with the first national guidelines published in 1925. See more on street signs in Chapter 5.

Early street and highway center lines were generally solid, but by the 1920s dashed lines were becoming more common (although some states continued to use solid lines much later). These dashed lines were white on two-lane roads, with yellow solid stripes on either side to indicate no-passing zones. Cities often used single white or yellow solid lines. Solid white lines on the edges of roads and traffic lanes became common by the 1950s.

In 1973 the standard was changed to yellow dashed lines, with white dashed lines separating multiple lanes traveling in the same direction. The recommended dimensions for dashed lines are 15-foot stripes with 25-foot gaps, but many variations can be found in practice, with shorter lines and gaps common in cities.

Other common markings in towns and cities include painted curbs indicating no-parking areas; parking lines (in many variations); turn lanes; crosswalk lines; and wide solid lines across a lane at stop signs or stoplights.

Lettering on pavement for streets and highways was specified in manuals by the 1940s. The most common

Pelle levels the plaster street by working it with a piece of thick styrene, The bottom is rounded slightly to give the street a slight crown. *Pelle Søeborg*

Lou Sassi prefers Dap Ready Mix concrete patch to simulate asphalt and concrete streets. The form is several layers of masking tape. *Lou Sassi*

include advance warnings for railroad ("R X R") and pedestrian crossings, as well as turn lane arrows and lettering (sometimes with route numbers).

Modeling materials

Many materials can be used to model streets and roads, including sheet styrene (plain and brick textured) cardstock, poured plaster, patching cement, spackle, foam sheets, and fine sand. There are also many commercial products, including in HO scale Walthers plastic street panels (simulated concrete, asphalt, and cobblestone), and HO and N concrete road sections from Rix Products. Flexible self-adhesive roadway sections from Walthers, SceneMaster,

Mini Highways, Faller, S&S Hobby Products, and Noch, are available plain or with highway markings. All can provide good results.

Chapter 3 discusses many of the considerations in planning and arranging city scenes, including blending streets, structures, track, and scenery. It's vital to have a good plan in place before starting street construction. Once you have a plan, match it with the materials you're comfortable with to re-create the specific type of streets you need.

A key with any material is having a smooth, solid base for the material. This can be plywood, foam, cork, or other material. Changes in grade should be smooth—abrupt changes will

not look realistic.

An entire book could be written on pavement modeling (and dozens of magazine articles have covered the topics)—space precludes detailed how-to instructions, but we'll take a look at the basics of using some common paving materials, adding grade crossings, and then see some methods of painting, weathering, and adding pavement markings. We'll close with a look at modeling trackage in streets.

Prefab and styrene streets and crossings

Walthers street panels are a great way to duplicate the look of city streets. They include pavement panels,

Lou paints his streets after the Ready Mix dries. He used stripwood as timbers on either side of each rail at his grade crossing, with paving material between. *Lou Sassi*

This brick street on John Pryke's HO Union Freight Railroad was modeled with Faller no. 601 brick paper, glued to styrene and matboard inserts cut to fit among the rails. The street in the distance is painted to represent concrete.
John Pryke

Walthers makes its HO street panels with a brick texture. The *Model Railroader* staff used these panels on its Milwaukee Road Beer Line project layout.
Jeff Wilson

the joints as tight as possible. Gaps are not as critical for concrete panels, as they can represent expansion joints. Glue the panels to the scenery base with latex construction adhesive.

Grade crossings can be done in many ways. Several companies offer grade-crossing kits for rubber-mat, concrete pad, and wood materials, including Blair Line; BLMA, now sold by Atlas; Walthers; and Woodland Scenics. Wood plank crossings were very common in towns and cities, with rubber-pad and concrete-pad crossings more common since the 1970s. Another common option was having guardrails or timbers inside the running rails, with paving material between the guardrails.

You can use commercial crossings, 7, or simulate wood crossings with scale stripwood. Either way the key is to make sure the top surface of the crossing material is slightly below the railheads to avoid catching a low-hanging uncoupling pin or pilot, and to make cleaning track less hazardous.

Streets and railroads sometimes cross at 90-degree angles, but other angles are more common. To make these crossings, simply cut the road material to match the angle of the crossing, 8.

I'm a big fan of sheet styrene for making asphalt and concrete streets. Sheets are available up to 4 x 8 feet (check plastic dealers and wholesalers in cities) making it easy to lay out large areas (including multiple blocks) on a single piece. Styrene is very versatile: the material is easy to cut, glue, and paint, and sheet styrene allows customizing street width and making curves and odd-angle intersections.

Start with a pattern: large sheets of craft paper work well, 9. For large flat areas, you can use the styrene as a sub-base under structures (more on that in Chapter 3). For most scenes, I make a sub-base of cork roadbed and sheets.

Transfer the outline of the streets to the styrene sheet, 10. I prefer .060" styrene, which is sturdy but still easy to cut. Trace along the line with a sharp hobby knife, then bend the plastic to snap it along the score.

Prep the plastic before gluing it in

sidewalks and curbing, as well as manhole cover and storm drain details. Advantages of using these include realistic crown and pavement textures/expansion joints, intersection pieces, and modular construction. The main disadvantages are the lack of curved sections—it can be difficult to fit odd-shaped spaces—and that only one street width is available. With a bit

of work, however, the pieces can be trimmed to create narrower streets or angled intersections.

Start by laying out pieces to match your structure arrangement, 6. Make sure you allow for sidewalks, clearance along rail lines, and other details. Start installing the panels at an intersection or key structure. Glue the panels together with plastic cement, making

Available materials include, from left, textured brick paper from Faller (17061) and Noch (56613), plastic from Vollmer (46028), flexible vinyl from Chooch (8620), and foam from Faller (170803). *Jeff Wilson*

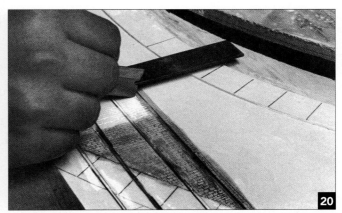

Walt Olsen is using a razor blade (a hobby knife would also work) and steel straightedge to carve plaster to represent bricks. Hand-carving bricks offers the most flexibility in design. *Walter R. Olsen*

place. Because styrene is very smooth, I like to add texture by sanding it. A piece of 160-grit sandpaper in a rubber sanding block works well. Use a circular motion and move along the surface until the plastic shine disappears. Joint lines (as with concrete) and cracks can easily be scored with a dental tool, **11**.

Once the styrene is in position, **12**, glue it to the base with latex contact cement, or a thin coat of latex construction adhesive.

Plaster and patching cement

Plaster also works well for creating streets. A key advantage is that it can follow curves and hills easily, and be customized for various street widths as well as parking lots and other paved areas. A key is to have a smooth, solid base for the material.

Add forms to make the outline for the street surface. This can be stripwood, strip styrene, thick tape (Woodland Scenics makes Paving Tape for this purpose), or layers of masking tape. Molding plaster (Woodland Scenics offers Smooth-It) should be mixed to a consistency of pancake batter, then poured into the form, as Pelle Søeborg is doing in **13**. (You can also color plaster with craft paint, powdered tempera paint, or masonry dye—the goal isn't necessarily to capture the final color of the road, but to tone down the white to hide any later chipping or cracking.)

Level and shape the material with a screed made of heavy sheet styrene,

Walt carved bricks only along the tracks, keeping the outside rows parallel to the rails. The bricks have a realistic, slightly uneven look. The layout is the HO scale Brandywine Transit Co. *Walter R. Olsen*

14. This can be slightly curved to allow for a crown in the roadway. Work the screed along the street with a slight back-and-forth motion. Work for a thickness of 1⁄16" to 1⁄8"—any thicker and the plaster will not dry properly, and will tend to crack.

When the plaster has set, remove the forms (don't wait until it dries completely or the edges may crack). Once the plaster has dried, sand any rough areas with fine sandpaper. This can be a dusty process—having a shop vacuum handy will help. Wiping the surface with a damp sponge can also work well, but the results will vary

Keys to realistic streets and roadways include realistic texture and color with neatly done, prototypical markings (including striping, arrows, and other details).

Pelle Søeborg

Streets can be brush-painted. Use a wide brush and go across the road surface.

Jeff Wilson

depending upon the exact plaster being used.

Modeler Lou Sassi uses a similar technique, but prefers concrete patching material (he uses Dap ReadyMix), **15**. The results look good, **16**. Other modelers have successfully used spackling compound or pre-mixed joint compound. These can all work, but are prone to cracking if applied too thickly. Another popular material, especially for smaller areas, is Durham's Water Putty.

With any of these materials, I highly recommend testing both the

material and method first before trying them on a finished scene.

Brick streets

Brick streets can be a challenge to model, but their detail can be eye-catching, **17**. A characteristic of most prototype brick streets is that bricks rarely follow perfect rows (or are identical in size and shape), and even when they do, after a few years of service individual bricks shift in position a bit. Most commercial brick materials are simply too regular in shape—they look *too* perfect.

A good starting point in HO is Walthers brick street panels, **18**. The challenge with them is to hide the seams between panels. Make them as tight as possible, filing or trimming any underlying material that prevents a tight joint.

Another viable option is brick sheet material, **19**, available in styrene, vinyl, and cardstock/paper from many sources including Walthers, JV Models, N Scale Architect, Plastruct, Vollmer, Chooch, Kibri, GC Laser, and Noch. These materials are textured and have varying patterns, which helps capture the irregular look of the real thing.

Use the largest pieces possible to minimize the number of visible seams. You can add some texture and vary the look of many styrene and vinyl brick sheets by scraping and scribing random bricks or creating new patterns with a hobby knife or dental pick.

Another method is pouring streets with plaster and hand-carving the bricks, **20**, with a hobby knife, razor blade, or dental pick. Although it might appear tedious, the method can yield excellent results, **21**. An advantage is that you can easily vary the brick pattern—for example, as in the photos, having the bricks outside the rail running perpendicular to the bricks inside the rails, and having the brick pattern naturally follow curves. Hand-carved bricks will also have a varied appearance that captures the look of the real thing.

Although an entire street would be time-consuming, capturing the look of a street where the brick only runs along the tracks (as with these images, where the rest of the street is asphalt) is a much more doable project.

Paint, markings, and weathering

Regardless of the paving material, painting it and adding striping and other markings are keys to realistic street modeling, **22**. Sloppy lines, improperly spaced striping, unprototypical markings, and unrealistic colors are all jarring visually and will kill the effect of an otherwise-dramatic scene.

The first step is applying a realistic base color. A challenge for simulating

A small foam roller can be used to paint large areas of streets or roadways. Flat house paint can be custom mixed to represent either asphalt or concrete. *Jeff Wilson*

Powdered chalk works well for weathering streets. A large brush makes it easier to get even results over long stretches of roadway. *Jeff Wilson*

either concrete or asphalt is that the surface, when viewed up close, is a mix of many colors. The best approach is usually to paint the surface a medium base color, then use various weathering techniques to provide the varied coloring effects. Regardless of the color or surface, make sure you use flat paint only—gloss, semi-gloss, eggshell, or satin paint finishes won't look realistic.

For concrete, it's tempting to reach for one of the model paints labeled "concrete." These can work for older concrete, but I've found lighter shades work well. My starting point is about a 2:2:1 mix of concrete, white, and light gray. The percentage isn't critical—test it and adjust as needed, adding more or less white depending on whether you're modeling newer or older concrete.

Asphalt varies even more in color. I usually start with a 2:1 mix of white and grimy black, adjusting again to find a tone close to the road I'm modeling.

Another option is to go to a paint store and get a custom-mixed pint or quart of the color you need. Grab a bunch of sample cards and put them on your layout (so you can choose the colors under the lighting in which they'll be viewed). This is a great option if you have a lot of street and road area to cover.

You can paint streets with a brush, **23**. Use a wide, soft brush and paint in full strokes across the street or road. Any brush marks will simply look like irregularities in the street surface. For large areas you can use a small foam roller, **24**.

Weathering can be done with an airbrush or brush. An airbrush is great for dusting on varied colors of gray or tan to vary the surface of the pavement, but you have to be aware of surroundings: Don't get overspray on adjoining scenery or structures (only use water-based paints, and provide ample ventilation).

I'm a fan of weathering chalks. Commercial weathering powders, such as those from AIM Products and Bar Mills, are handy and work well. I also keep artist's chalks handy (a set of basic colors and a set of various gray shades)—it's easy to make your own powder from these by scraping them with a hobby knife.

Traffic lanes typically show darker wear patterns down the middle of the lanes, but on some surfaces, the areas where tires travel will appear darker. You can add these with a brush, **25**. I find a large brush (like the standard 2"-wide paintbrush in the photo) works best for creating a consistent, even effect. For smaller areas, or to simulate patches of fluid leaks and droppings, you can simply use a finger, makeup sponge, or small brush. A small brush is also good for re-creating tar patch lines, **26**, and the separating lines between concrete panels.

Brick presents a different challenge. Most paving bricks are dark red to brown, but the color of individual stones can vary slightly, **27**. Some brick paper may already have this appearance. For textured styrene bricks, start with a uniform base color (various boxcar red or brown shades work well), then use

Tar patches can be simulated with black paint (brushed on or with a paint marker). A pencil works well for drawing small cracks. *Jeff Wilson*

a fine brush to paint individual bricks lighter and darker shades.

You can highlight the seams by brushing dark gray powdered chalk across the surface using a large brush. Work the chalk into the texture, then finish with soft strokes along the surface or wipe the surface with your finger or a cloth. The result will be a varied appearance that highlights the seams among bricks.

Many brick streets, like the one in **27**, were patched with asphalt. You can capture this by adding patching material (plaster, water putty, or simply epoxy) and painting it to represent asphalt.

Striping can be done in several ways. Check prototype photos and various editions of the *Manual on Uniform Traffic Control Devices* (MUTCD) for guidelines on appropriate colors,

Paving bricks could vary quite a bit in color as shown in this 1955 view from Philadelphia. Also note the asphalt patch to the right. *C. Houser; Krambles-Peterson archives*

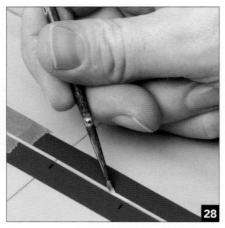

To paint road striping, start by masking the area. I marked the beginning and end points of the dashed stripes on the tape. *Jeff Wilson*

markings, and stripe widths and placement.

You can add markings using paint, dry transfers, chalk, or colored tape. My favorites are paint, chalk, and dry transfers. Some modelers have used pinstriping and other colored tape. I find this looks good from a distance, but up close the tape's thickness is apparent.

To paint lines, start by masking the area, **28**. Make sure the edges are burnished firmly to the surface. For dashed lines, you can fully mask the individual stripes or do as I did and just mark their start and end points on the tape.

Paint the stripe with a fine brush. Neither white nor yellow are known for covering well, so you can use this to your advantage by applying a single coat for a worn look, or use multiple coats for better coverage.

Chalk is an effective way to duplicate the look of faded striping. Mask the stripe as before, then use either a stiff brush (hog bristle works well) to rub white or yellow powdered chalk on the surface, or simply use a stick of chalk or an artist's pencil. As long as this is done on a flat-finish surface, I've found there's no need to seal the chalk with a clear coat.

Dry transfer striping is available in white and yellow in a variety of widths. Its advantages are that it will have a consistent width, a consistent color, and no masking is required. It will look like a newly painted line.

Place the transfer sheet over the paving surface, making sure it is precisely aligned. Use a burnishing tool to rub the backing sheet until you see the color change, then rub harder to secure the transfer to the surface, **29**.

For dashed lines, use a hobby knife to slice the stripes to the appropriate lengths on the backing sheet. Use a template or scale rule to ensure consistent spacing between stripes. Following exact prototype spacing can look long on modeled scenes because of perspective, so shortening the stripes

and spacing a bit will look realistic.

You can also use fine-point paint markers to make stripes, **30**. A key is to use a guide for the marker: a heavy rule or straightedge and an artist's french curve. Use even pressure and keep the marker going at a steady pace. This technique requires a steady hand—practice first before using it on a finished street.

Several companies make templates for highway markings, including the common "RR XING" warning. You can also make your own templates of these from paper or thin cardboard by following patterns from the MUTCD or other sources, **31**. Either use these directly for masking, or trace the outline on the road, mask the area, and paint the markings.

Sidewalks

City sidewalks are as important as the streets themselves. Walthers offers sidewalks with its street panel kits and as a separate item. Sidewalks, including curbing, is also available from Bar Mills, Bachmann, Chooch, Downtown Deco, Faller, JTT Miniature Tree, Kibri, Smalltown USA, and others. Another good option is styrene sheet from Evergreen, which is available with a tile pattern in various sizes. Sidewalks can also be cast in plaster as with streets, or made from sheets of plain styrene with expansion joints scored in the surface.

Make sure sidewalks are wide enough to allow for details and figures. A width of 6 to 10 scale feet usually looks reasonable. An option is continuing the sidewalk material underneath structures to provide a base—more on that in Chapter 3.

Tracks in the street

Railroad tracks and streets have used shared rights-of-way since the mid-1800s, **32**. Street trackage was quite common through the early 1900s, including streetcar (and heavier interurban) electric lines and standard (steam) railroads. Although it is much more rare today, you can still find prototype examples across the country.

Streetcar lines were found in cities of all sizes (and even in some smaller

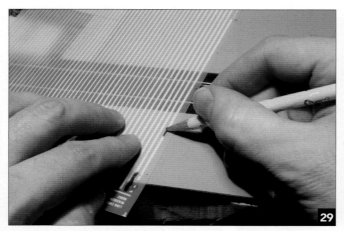

Dry-transfer striping can be used on streets. For dashed lines, cut the striping on the sheet before applying. Use a pencil or burnishing tool to firmly apply the transfers. *Jeff Wilson*

With a fine-point paint marker, use a guide such as this draftsman's french curve as David Popp is doing here on his N scale New Haven layout. *David Popp*

Pelle Søeborg created stencils on the computer, transferring the markings with pencil to the street (left). He used the markings to mask the areas on the road, then used a brush to paint the design (right). *Two photos: Pelle Søeborg*

towns) from the 1880s through the 1930s—later in some areas. Streetcars didn't require track built to steam-railroad standards, so they were built with lighter rail, tighter curves, and steeper grades compared to standard railroad construction. Chapter 7 goes into detail on these lines.

Steam railroads shared city streets in cities and smaller towns alike. This could mean a main line trundling the entire length of a town or a few blocks in a street in a city. Many cities had switching lines through industrial areas that wound among multiple streets and private rights-of-way, **33**.

A variation in some cities was having the track not in the pavement but directly next to the street, or running down the middle of a boulevard, with paved streets on either side, **34**.

Construction

Track in pavement is laid and secured, **35**, before paving material is added. Conventional track could have rails spiked or bolted to ties; streetcar track was often laid with steel tie bars between the rails to hold the gauge (especially on tight curves). Paving material is then added to rail-top level, so that vehicles can smoothly cross rails as with a railroad grade crossing.

Keeping flangeways clear is important. Streetcar lines were often laid with girder rail, which has a built-in flangeway, **36**. Street tracks on steam railroads and many streetcar

and interurban lines were also built with standard rail as well, often with guardrails inside the running rails, with heavier rail for standard railroads.

Rail is classified by weight in pounds per yard. In the early 1900s, most railroads were using at least 90-pound rail (standing 5⅜" tall), with heavier rail on high-traffic lines, while streetcar and interurban lines typically used 55- or 60-pound rail (4¹⁄₁₆" and 4¼" tall).

Turnouts in pavement require special treatment. Along with ensuring that the point rails can move freely, special throw mechanisms are needed: A conventional switch stand couldn't be used, as it would interfere with vehicular traffic, **37**. The switch stand handle was located in a depressed area

A New York Central passenger train rolls down Washington Street in Syracuse, N.Y., in 1936. The main line was relocated north of the city later that year. *Trains magazine collection*

A Detroit Transit Railroad switcher pulls several cars down some undulating track in a worn brick street in Detroit in May 1980. *Byron C. Babbish*

Here's the fireman's view from an F unit cab as a Rock Island westbound travels down Fifth Street in Davenport, Iowa, in the 1960s. The double-track main divided the street. *Philip A. Weibler*

either between or along the rails with a hinged cover that was normally closed to allow vehicle traffic over it. Crews generally used hooks to open these covers—these areas were found cozy by rats, snakes, and other critters.

Street track could be found in any type of paving material: asphalt, concrete, or brick, or combination: with timbers along and between rails, or brick or concrete along rails and asphalt for the rest of the street.

Design

As you can imagine, combining rail traffic with automobiles and trucks often didn't always go well. Along with vehicular traffic that didn't always yield to trains, other problems included vehicles parking on rails or within restricted clearance areas. Along main streets, stoplights were triggered by approaching trains so that side streets received stop signals.

Track in pavement is also a

maintenance headache: replacing a broken rail or making any other repair requires digging up the paving, and it is similarly difficult to make any modifications in track. Vehicles added wear and tear to the track structure, and gravel and debris in flangeways (or ice in winter) needed to be cleared. Trains likewise caused damage to streets, with passing trains eventually cracking paving materials.

Streetcar tracks often ran in pairs, with one line in each traffic lane matching the direction of travel wherever possible. Railroad and interurban lines, however, often headed down the center of the street on a single track.

When it came to industrial tracks, there was no such thing as "common" or "typical." In the era where heavy industries were concentrated in the middle of large cities, railroads used a mix of private rights-of-way and running along and through streets. You'll see more examples in Chapters 3 and 4. Industrial track often has many tight clearances, sharp curves, and crossings.

Modeling street tracks

As with real railroads, a key in successfully modeling street trackage is to make sure your initial trackwork operates flawlessly before paving the street. As you design each scene, minimize turnouts in pavement as much as possible—you'll be thankful later.

The easiest approach is to use standard track components (flextrack, sectional track, and prefab turnouts). It's not necessary, but I recommend soldering all rail joints in street trackage and using all-live turnouts (avoid power-routing turnouts that rely on switch points contacting stock rails to get power). This will minimize chances of electrical contact issues over time.

Even if the rest of your layout uses manual turnout controls, consider using under-table switch machines, such as Circuitron's Tortoise (or a manual remote-control system), for turnouts in pavement. This minimizes the risks of reaching into scenes among buildings to throw turnouts.

Once your trackwork is complete, run LOTS of trains—run all types of equipment you plan to use, all lengths of cars, and run them forward and backward through all turnout routes until they operate perfectly. Fix all problem areas before adding paving.

The easiest way to model track in street is with Walthers HO prefab street track inserts, **38** (Kato and TomyTec make street track and inserts in N scale). Photo **2** shows some of this in use. The set includes pre-made turnout inserts (for no. 4 and 18"-radius turnouts) and for 15"-, 18"-, and 22"-radius curves.

You can also make your own street sections to fit around the track, using styrene sheet or matboard. That's how John Pryke made the street scene in **17**. Cut pieces to fit among rails, **39**. You can use paper templates (press paper in place atop the rails to form them), then cut them out and use them to make the finished pieces. Turnout pieces can be duplicated from a master. Use plastic putty or filler to smooth seams between sections and fill any gaps between street pieces and the outsides of rails.

Street trackage is being built in Austin, Texas, in the 1960s. The ties are being laid on a bed of asphalt on crushed rock; rail has been installed in the background. Note the multiple round smudge-pot warning flares. *Dryden L. Prentice*

Streetcar track often used girder rail, which had built-in guardrails, as here in this under-construction photo from Memphis, Tenn., in 1906. The track is in; paving will soon be added to railtop level. *Library of Congress*

The control handle for this switch is between the points. This is in Yakima, Wash., in 1985. *Jigger Schmidt, Historic American Engineering Record*

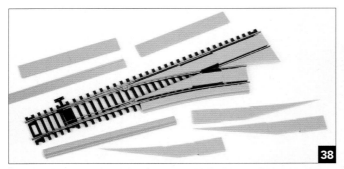

38

Walthers makes HO injection-molded street-track insert kits, including pieces to fit in turnouts. They can be used with its street panels or other materials. *Jeff Wilson*

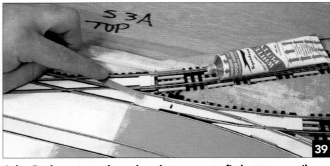

39

John Pryke cut matboard and styrene to fit between rails. He filled the gaps between sections with putty. Stripwood supports the street at the proper height. *John Pryke*

40

Allow enough of a flangway for smooth operation. John painted and weathered this section of street to represent old concrete, with different types near the rails and between sections. *John Pryke*

41

Street track can be simulated with poured plaster. Here Pelle Søeborg is using a plastic screed to level the plaster at railtop height. Flangeways will be cut when the plaster sets. *Pelle Søeborg*

42

Rails are realistically set in the pavement at this industrial area. Check flangeways with equipment to make sure everything runs smoothly. *Pelle Søeborg*

43

Street running is a key part of the Carroll Street industrial area on Paul Dolkos's HO scale layout. Paul used Orr girder rail and custom-laser-cut brick sections. *Paul Dolkos*

Stripwood or strip styrene glued to the sub-base and ties brings the level of the street sections even (the top of the pavement should be just below the top of the rail).

Allow enough of a flangeway gap inside the running rails so that rolling stock operates smoothly. You can add guardrails inside the running rails if desired. John's finished, weathered

street is shown in **40**.

You can also model track in pavement by pouring streets from plaster as described earlier. Make sure the plaster is level with the rail tops, **41**. Flangeways can be cut when the plaster sets using a hobby knife. You can also use guardrails or timbers (stripwood) along the inner rails, and stripwood to simulate timbers around turnouts.

Street trackage, whether part of an electric line or standard railroad, can be an eye-catching element of a model railroad, **43**. Experiment with various paving and track techniques until you find one that works well for you.

1

Urban structures and scenery

Planning model railroad scenery for city scenes is much different than for rural areas. It's entirely possible for structures, streets, sidewalks, and retaining walls to make up the entire scene, with no (or minimal) grassy areas or other traditional scenic contours, **1**.

A Chicago Great Western switcher pulls a transfer caboose and freight cars along street trackage among warehouse buildings in the Kansas City Bottoms in April 1965. For many modelers, the goal of modeling urban areas is to capture the look of industrial switching lines. *Louis A. Marre collection*

33

A Baltimore & Ohio tank engine moves cars along street trackage among storefront and industrial structures. The Severna Park Model Railroad Club's HO layout features a lot of city modeling based on Baltimore. *Paul J. Dolkos*

To use structure photos as flats, edit images with the "skew" tool (this is Photoshop Elements) to straighten walls and other features. *Jeff Wilson*

Poster prints work well for outputting photos of structure walls. Conventional matte photo paper or light cardstock can also be used. *Jeff Wilson*

This can be a good thing if re-creating hillsides, trees, and grassy meadows isn't your favorite modeling activity. Urban modeling has its own special appeal, **2**; it does, however, present its own challenges in realistically arranging and blending scenic elements while keeping trackwork accessible for maintenance and operation.

Prototype cities and towns have many types of structures. For the most part, in modeling them we concentrate on structures near the tracks: Retail buildings and blocks, industries, stations (Chapter 6 looks at passenger terminals), freight houses, crossing towers, interlocking towers, and the like. Although significant and dominating, high-rise office buildings and skyscrapers are usually best left to be represented as distant buildings on backdrops with photos. Houses and residential areas are also not as prominent (except where tracks run behind residential neighborhoods).

Entire books and hundreds of magazine articles have discussed structure construction and detailing (my book *Modeling Structures*, published by Kalmbach in 2015, is a good start), so we'll focus more on how to plan groups of structures, how to layer structures and building flats with photo backdrops to make realistic scenes, and how to effectively plant buildings and blend them with streets, trackwork, and scenery. We'll also look at tips and tricks like using mirrors and

Images can be glued directly to the backdrop (background) or to mat board or foam core for use as flats. *Jeff Wilson*

making buildings, flats, and backdrops with photos of real structures.

Photo backdrops and flats

The wide availability of photo-editing software such as Adobe Photoshop and its less-expensive cousin, Photoshop Elements, has made it much easier to create realistic customized backdrop images and structure flats. Several manufacturers also offer backdrops that can be used for backdrops and flats; some, such as railroadbackdrops.com, will customize them for you.

I keep my camera handy when traveling, and I'm constantly taking photos of buildings and signs that I think might be good candidates for turning into models. Many older

buildings are still standing, so even if you model the steam era, you can, with a bit of photo editing, produce structure flats that will work on your layout.

When taking photos for this, get as square to the side of the structure as possible. If you can, get back far enough to use a 50mm or longer lens, as wider-angle lenses can create distortion and curved lines. Fill the frame if possible; otherwise take

This structure is a styrene shell with a photo print of a laundromat on the front and a wall from another structure on the side. *Jeff Wilson*

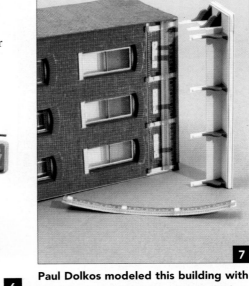

Paul Dolkos modeled this building with a print of a real building, but built the windows in layers, then added a three-dimensional cornice. *Paul J. Dolkos*

Blocks of storefront buildings are common to cities and towns alike, with the main difference the height of the buildings. This HO scene has a mix of buildings, with Walthers street and sidewalk sections. *Jeff Wilson*

The angled street at right keeps viewers from looking down and seeing the backdrop. Bob and Bev Shea did the HO modeling, which also features a retaining wall capped with fences and several layers of buildings and flats. *John Pryke*

multiple photos, moving down the structure, so you can blend them later digitally. For later photo blending, keep the camera the same distance from the building with the same lens/focal length and camera settings.

The first thing you'll have to do with editing software is to straighten the image, making sure that edges are parallel and corners are square, **3**. The "skew" function works well for this. You can also adjust the lighting and remove and modify details (on that image I removed wires hanging in front of the building). Changes can include adding/removing/modifying windows and doors, altering signs (you can add a 1950s sign over a modern one, for example), modifying the height and length, and combining multiple structures.

The resulting images can be printed with a home printer on heavy paper, light cardstock (be aware of what works best in your printer), or matte photo paper. I've also had success printing larger inexpensive poster prints, **4**.

Rick Van Laar built this city using a line of full-size structures, with two rows of shallow-relief buildings at rear. Buildings hide the end of the road at left; the street at right ends in a T. *Lou Sassi*

Earl Smallshaw ran this urban street into a commercial print on the backdrop. The railroad bridge and overhead structure help hide the joint. *Earl Smallshaw*

The distant flag, round planter, and street buildings are actually reflections in a mirror (the top of which is disguised by the banner) on Gerry Leone's HO layout. *Gerry Leone*

Here's the scene that is reflected in the mirror—the photo image is hidden on the rear of a structure just around the bend in the street at right in photo 12.
Gerry Leone

These (I use shortrunposters.com) are much cheaper than photo prints, and although their detail isn't quite as sharp, I've found them more than acceptable for modeling. With these, you can print large building sides, or have several sides on the same print.

The resulting prints can be mounted directly to the backdrop, or to make flats, on mat board, foam core, or Gator Board, **5**. I use spray adhesive; you can use latex contact cement as well, but make sure to apply it in thin coats.

You can take this a step further by applying a photo print to part of a three-dimensional building or make an entire building with photo prints, **6**. Secure the prints to a solid shell made of styrene or foam core. Clear acrylic sheet works well, especially for large buildings, and allows the option of cutting out window openings to reveal "glass."

You can enhance these printed flats and walls by adding a few three-dimensional details to them, such as signs, awnings, and fire escapes, **7**. This can be especially effective for buildings that are close to foregrounds.

Retail blocks

Blocks of storefront structures and retail buildings can be found in towns and cities alike, **8**. These can be straightforward, in a conventional layout with connecting streets at 90-degree angles, or complex, with curved streets, streets on hills, or intersections at odd angles.

Prototype blocks are quite long in model terms, with typical sizes in the U.S. ranging from about 250 to 400 feet long (about 3 to 5 actual feet for HO scale). We can use selective compression to shorten these considerably on layouts—having four or five typical storefront buildings between side streets is enough to capture the feel of a city block. The main differences between towns and cities will be the height of buildings and the amount of traffic, as Chapter 1 explained. The basic modeling techniques for each will be similar.

In planning, try various combinations of structures for the best overall effect. You can always add a vacant lot between buildings if you're locked into a specific block length but individual building widths don't add up.

Keep in mind hiding side streets that go to your backdrop. There are a few tricks to enable this. Angling or curving the street so it goes behind other buildings is one method, **9**. You can have the side street end at a T in front of building flats or prints on the backdrop; you can layer additional flats to simulate the feel of a larger city, or a city on a hill, **10**.

If you run a street directly into a backdrop, you can use a photo print on the backdrop to make it look like the street and buildings continue, **11**. The challenge with this method is perspective: It's possible to align a print of a street continuation so that it looks good from one vantage point (usually looking directly down the street), but as soon as the viewing angle shifts, the perspective view no longer aligns. The deeper the scene, the easier it is to do

This shows the mirror and structures being tested in position prior to scenery being added. The building hiding the photo doesn't yet have a roof. *Gerry Leone*

The front of this building rests on an extension of the sidewalk; the rear on styrene strip. The hole is for wire access for lighting. *Jeff Wilson*

this (as a viewer moving left or right will be blocked by 3-D structures).

Also, when doing this, make sure the colors blend well between the street and sidewalk and the matching backdrop image. The joint can be partially hidden by items like vehicles, bridges, and other details.

Mirrors can be used to hide the ends of streets or tracks, and can also expand the apparent space being used. A city street scene on Gerry Leone's old HO Bona Vista layout illustrates this well, **12**. Gerry combined an angled mirror at the end of the street with a photo print hidden behind a

structure to make it appear that the street extended much farther than the backdrop, **13**, **14**.

Mirrors come in two types: Front-surface and rear-surface (conventional) reflecting. Front-surface mirrors are more expensive, but it's easier to hide the joint between mirror and scenery. Experiment with mirrors when planning and placing mirrors to determine the best locations. The key is that viewers should never be able to see themselves in a mirror on a layout.

In planting storefront structures, it's important to keep them level, so that there's no gap between the bottom of

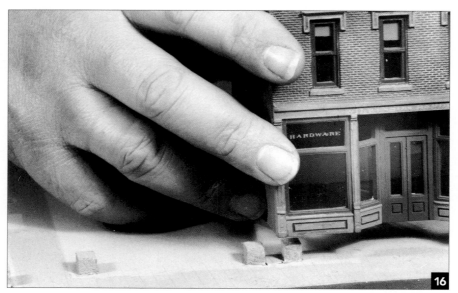

Small wood or styrene blocks glued to the layout will keep structures aligned without having to glue them in place. *John Pryke*

the building and the sidewalk. I like to extend the sidewalk material under the front of the building, **15**. You can use strip or sheet styrene to support the rear and sides of structures.

As Chapter 2 suggested, it's wise to paint and weather the streets and sidewalks before adding structures. I like to use a small drop of super glue at each corner to secure each structure. This holds the building securely, but makes it easy to remove it later if needed. You can also simply set structures in place—this simplifies cleaning and repairs—but it's easy to inadvertently bump a building (or row of buildings) out of position. To remedy this, John Pryke uses small blocks as alignment posts, **16**. This keeps buildings in position without glue.

Another installation method is to build structures in larger subassemblies before adding them to the layout. You can do this with entire blocks, as Gerry Leone did on his Bona Vista, **17**. The entire block is mounted on a large styrene sheet (available from plastics dealers), which—after expansion joints have been scored—also serves as the sidewalk and curb. This can be done directly on the layout as well, but working on assemblies at your workbench usually provides better light and access. It's a great technique especially for special situations, such as odd-shaped blocks or streets on hills.

You can also do this for smaller assemblies—such as individual buildings, small groups of structures, or an industrial complex.

Structures along hilly streets require care during installation. Make sure that each structure is level and the walls vertical, **18**. Place each structure on its own styrene base, with edges painted concrete to match the sidewalk color, then align it so the entryway matches the sidewalk. If the structure is slightly taller, there can be a step down from the structure's entry door to the sidewalk. You can add steps or contour pieces of strip styrene at the doorway as well.

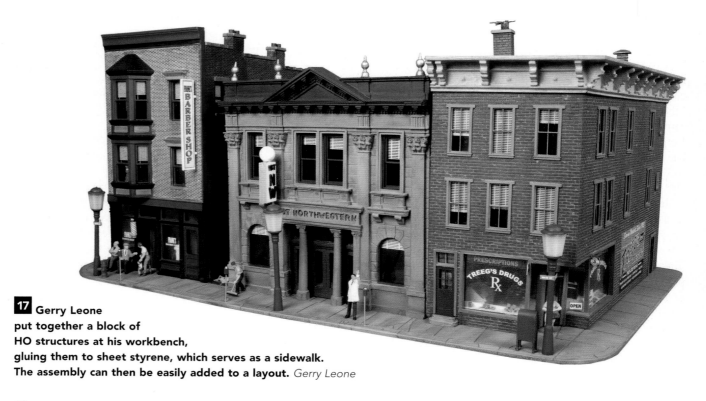

17 Gerry Leone
put together a block of
HO structures at his workbench,
gluing them to sheet styrene, which serves as a sidewalk.
The assembly can then be easily added to a layout. *Gerry Leone*

Note the varying levels of the structures along the sidewalk on the hill. Make sure each structure is level, with walls vertical. David Popp did the modeling on his N scale New Haven layout. *David Popp*

Industrial scenes

For many modelers, "urban modeling" implies industrial areas, manufacturing plants, and tall buildings surrounding tracks. This can mean industrial tracks and spurs wandering in streets and tight spaces among these buildings, **19**, or main lines cutting behind a variety of big structures, **20**. Chapter 4 shows more details of railroad rights-of-way.

Incorporating these scenes into a layout can be done in different ways, **21**. Look for prototype scenes that have long, tall structures that can be modeled along a backdrop, **22**. By using shallow-relief structures and building flats, this type of scene can be modeled convincingly even on a narrow shelf while having easy access to what can be complex trackwork, **23**.

Many industrial areas feature tracks curving sharply between buildings, **24**, and into tight areas. These buildings were often built with curved and angled walls specifically to accommodate rail sidings. These spur tracks and sidings don't have to be long to capture the feel of the prototype, and even spurs that handle two or three cars will provide lots of operational interest.

Mocking up these areas full size can help visualize how all of the elements—backdrop, flats, 3-D structures, and trackwork—will come together, **25**. Tracks at angles also help mask joints with the backdrop, as do additional structure walls or flats at the ends of these spurs.

An important factor in realistic city and town scenes is controlling the observer's viewpoint: Looking down on scenes like these can kill the realism, as it becomes apparent that flats and shallow-relief structures aren't really buildings. Realism is greatly enhanced if you can position the layout (and scenes) at eye level, so the viewer's eye is level with (or even slightly below) track level.

Planting industrial structures is a matter of blending streets, parking areas (paved and gravel), grass, and trackwork (including ballast). Make sure the structure sits level on a firm base. Then, once basic scenic materials are down, matte medium can be brushed along the structure's base, with ground foam, gravel, or other material applied, **26**. If you're trying to simulate pavement abutting the structure, fill any gaps with thick super glue, then paint it to match the paving.

This 1950s industrial scene on the Chicago & North Western in Chicago has complex trackwork with a crossing running right through a turnout, and a wood plank alleyway nestled among tall city structures. *Keith Kohlmann collection*

Remember that track is part of the scenery as well. Track should have a difference in appearance depending on whether it is a main line, secondary track, or industrial spur, and whether it sees frequent or seldom use. (Chapter 4 goes into detail about track variations.) Vary ballast colors, including grass- and weed-covered track. When modeling foliage on track, make sure rails are clear of any obstacles.

Open ground around and among buildings in urban areas is sometimes grass, or simply weeds and overgrowth, or dirt and gravel. In any case, these areas can be modeled by coating them with Sculptamold, plaster, or other

traditional scenic base materials, then painting the base an earth color and adding real dirt, ground foam, static grass, weeds, and scenic tufts as needed.

Freight houses

Freight houses were signature structures in large cities, **27**. Through the steam and early diesel eras, railroads handled a great deal of less-than-carload (LCL)—also called "merchandise" or "package"—traffic. Parcels were gathered at smaller stations, consolidated at larger city terminals, and then shipped throughout the country on boxcars that were scheduled

as tightly as passenger cars and trains.

City freight houses, which were usually near major freight yards, could handle 100 to 200 boxcars of LCL traffic every day, making them among the railroads' busiest switching locations. Modeling one realistically can take a lot of space, but can be rewarding operationally.

Railroads' LCL traffic began dropping dramatically in the 1950s as trucking companies took over most package business; by the mid-1960s most railroad freight houses were closed, and railroads were out of the LCL business completely by the early 1970s.

Coming out of Milwaukee's downtown, the Milwaukee Road main line passed through industrial areas featuring tight trackwork in pavement, with spurs to nearby buildings. The scene is from 1973. *Ray Szopieray, courtesy Milwaukee County Historical Society*

Bill Denton did a masterful job of modeling the Milwaukee Road's Kingsbury Street (Chicago) branch in N scale. Note the detailing on the track, streets, and structures. *Bill Denton*

A Milwaukee Road switcher works boxcars of grain at the elevators in Minneapolis on February 2, 1959. Industrial areas with long, tall buildings are ideal for modeling. *William D. Middleton*

22

23

Logan Holtgrewe modeled an industrial area of Baltimore on the Severna Park club's HO layout. The brewery and other buildings are based on specific prototypes. *Paul J. Dolkos*

Crossing gates, shanties, and towers

Grade crossings in towns and cities offer a wealth of potential details, including signs, signals, gates, and vehicles. Manually controlled crossing gates, together with attendants' towers and shanties, were common elements of urban railroad scenes from the late 1800s through the 1950s, **28**. A crossing watchman holding a stop sign was sufficient for low-traffic areas, but in cities, with high volumes of street vehicle traffic, combined with busy rail lines (often with multiple tracks), more protection was needed.

The solution was to add crossing gates that could be controlled manually by an operator, **29**. A heavy cast pedestal at the side of the road served as a mounting point for the gate. The gate arm was made up of two separate pieces, joined at the free end and separated so that one piece mounted on either side of the pedestal. The gate itself was wood, designed to be thin and light enough so that if a car hit it, it would break or shatter, keeping the mechanism from being damaged.

One or two counterweights were placed on the pivot end of the gate. These balanced the weight of the gate, lessening the effort needed to raise and lower the gate. A rod, hung from the free end of the gate, swung freely down as the gate was lowered. This served as a stop, keeping the end of the gate from swinging too far down and contacting the ground.

Where gates protected city streets with sidewalks, the pedestal would be located between the street and sidewalk. A separate small arm to protect the sidewalk could then be mounted on the opposite side of the pedestal.

Gates were painted with diagonal black-and-white or red-and-white stripes to increase visibility. At many locations, stop signs were hung on the gates in the daytime. Red lanterns were hung on the gates at night. Both of these were tasks done by the crossing watchman.

Most manual gate installations relied on four gates: Two on each side of the road and two on each side of the tracks. Each gate covered the near lane of the road, so that together the two gates on the same side of the tracks completely blocked off the road. This was done to discourage drivers from trying to beat a train to a crossing by driving around a single gate.

Early gates were controlled mechanically. When a train approached, the watchman operated the lever or crank to lower the gates, then flagged the intersection with a stop sign until the train cleared. He would then raise the gates.

These mechanisms wouldn't always operate smoothly—especially in the winter, when ice could build up in many areas. If the gates couldn't be lowered, the watchman would have to simply flag the crossing with a sign or lantern. The controls for early mechanical gates were often located on the ground outside of a crossing shanty, but elevated towers, **30**, became more common for later installations.

Pneumatic (air-powered) gates soon became the standard for most manual crossing installations. They were easily controlled from an elevated tower and they were more reliable, as air lines could be run to multiple gates and for longer distances, allowing a single operator to control gates at multiple crossings.

Some manual crossings received electrically powered gates, but for the most part, the coming of electric gates meant the installation of automatic signals and gates triggered by track circuits. All-electric installations (gates and flashers) were sometimes still controlled by watchmen on site, especially at busy city intersections. The main reason was that an operator could better adjust the timing of the warning devices based on train speeds (especially when controlling multiple crossings), lessening street congestion.

Following World War II, most manually controlled crossings were converted. Several manual crossings survived into the 1950s; by the 1960s most were gone, although a few made it as late as the 2000s.

Elevated towers were common in cities and other high-traffic areas, especially if a single operator controlled more than one grade crossing. Towers provided watchmen a good view of approaching trains and automobiles as well as the surrounding area.

Crossing towers generally followed standard designs of the railroads that owned them. Crossing towers were smaller than interlocking towers, and although many had enclosed lower stories (often used for storing spare parts and tools), it was common for the bottom to simply be open, with a metal or wood framework supporting

the elevated operator's cabin with an outside staircase or ladder for access.

A bell was usually mounted directly outside the tower. Many were manual, requiring the operator to pull a rope to ring the bell (watchmen became adept at ringing the bell while operating the gate mechanism). Many were eventually converted to electric bells. Other details include a coal bin for a

24

Warehouses and industrial buildings were often built with curved and angled walls to match spur tracks. The track curves into the building at center. Guardrails are common on tightly curved track. *Trains magazine collection*

25

Test-fitting structures, track, background photos and flats, and other elements will help create more-realistic scenes. *Paul J. Dolkos*

26

Make sure buildings are firmly "planted." A bead of matte medium around the structure base, with ground foam, grass, ballast, and dirt, will hide joints. Cinders and weeds cover the ties of the spur. *Jeff Wilson*

City freight houses handled large amounts of less-than-carload (LCL) freight through the early diesel era. The Erie's Chicago 14th Street freight house, tucked near the Erie freight yard, could handle 100 merchandise boxcars on its seven parallel tracks (plus a couple dozen trucks). *Erie*

The crossing tender has lowered the gates and is watching the train near his shelter at left. Grade crossings offer lots of detail. Two streetcar tracks also cross, with a streetcar waiting in the distance. Also note the period vehicles, signs, streetlights, and line poles. *Missouri Pacific*

This busy double-track crossing has double gates on each side. The operator's controls are outside, next to the shelter at right. Note the wood plank crossings with bricks between. *New York Central*

stove, a portable stop sign hanging on a wall or stand, and a shed for tools, spare parts, and lanterns.

For modeling, you could easily scratchbuild some of the simpler designs. Walthers has offered assembled elevated crossing towers with gates in HO and N scales, as well as crossing shanties. Other companies making towers and shanties include American Model Builders, Atlas, BTS, JL Innovative Design, Micron Art, and Scale Structures Ltd.

For crossing gates, in HO Walthers has manually operated pneumatic gates and NJ International has more modern electric gates with two arm styles in HO and N. Bachmann has a set of manual gates in HO (No. 42200) and N (No. 42504) that, although toy-like, are inexpensive and can be the basis for a kitbashing project with new arms.

Towers could remain standing for years after automatic devices were installed; if you model a more modern period, a tower with boarded-up

windows and a nearby relay cabinet can show that the crossing was once controlled manually. Likewise, shanties often stood after crossings were automated, used for tool, parts, or material storage.

Finishing
Remember that modeling cities is largely a matter of finding individual prototype scenes, then connecting them to create a realistic overall effect. Look to the prototype for inspiration, concentrating on the era, region, or specific city and railroad you're modeling.

We've looked at streets and structures; the next chapter takes a look at the railroad right-of-way itself, and Chapter 5 shows many options for detailing urban scenes, including signs of many types.

Towers gave watchmen a better view of oncoming trains and vehicles. This tower controls pneumatic gates on the Pennsylvania at Williamsport, Pa., in the 1940s. *A.C. Kalmbach*

CHAPTER FOUR

Along the urban right-of-way

Instead of hills, mountains, and prairies, the railroad right-of-way in urban areas passes through scenery of structures, retaining walls, and streets. Complex trackwork, a lack of ballast, tight curves, and tall buildings are all hallmarks of city railroading, and are apparent in this 1930 view.
Trains magazine collection

We've looked at the streets, structures, and other components in city scenes, but what of the railroad track itself? Trackwork in urban areas tends to be more complex, with bridges, junctions, tight clearances, additional tracks, and multiple routes, **1**. A right-of-way in a large city should definitely have a different look than a rail line in the country.

Rails are spiked in place on tie plates, with joint bars bolted to rails to secure them end-to-end. The bond wire ensures solid electrical contact for signals. *H. Reid*

A switchman throws a lever on a manual switch stand in Chicago & North Western's Proviso (Chicago) Yard in the early 1940s. No ballast here—just cinders, and the near track has only a couple of tie plates. *John Vachon, Library of Congress*

Capturing the varied look of the track, roadbed, and other components are important in realistically re-creating city scenes. We'll start with a look at some basics of track, ballast, and roadbed, including features that make city track unique. We'll then examine features such as junctions, bridges, retaining walls, and other elements of city and town rights-of-way.

Track basics

The track structure consists of steel rails that rest atop wood or concrete ties. This in turn rests on roadbed—usually ballast—atop graded earth. Although seemingly simple, track takes on many appearances depending upon rail size, use, depth of ballast, and how well it's maintained—urban areas have a broad mix of well-maintained main lines, weedy spurs, track in pavement, and seldom-used tracks buried in earth or foliage.

Prototype rail comes in many sizes, creating a distinctive appearance as it varies by height and the width of its base. Rail is classified based on its weight per yard. Modern mainline track is the heaviest, running from about 116 pounds to 132 pounds per yard (about 7¼" tall). In the early 1900s, when

Industrial and spur tracks are often weed-grown. Bumpers like this (two ties across the rails) are typical for seldom-used tracks. *Trains magazine collection*

locomotives and rolling stock were lighter, 90-pound (5⅜" tall) to 112-pound rail was common for main lines. Lighter rail is used for industrial spurs and other secondary trackage (such as industrial branches in cities).

This variance in rail height can be captured on model railroads as well, as manufacturers offer track in various sizes. For example, in HO, you can model main lines with code 83 track components (rail .083" tall, representing 132-pound rail) and secondary tracks with code 70 (.070" tall rail, 100-pound rail) or code 55

Note the variance in tie colors along this spur track. The fine gravel roadbed looks gray, but there are lots of variations in the aggregate colors as well. *Jeff Wilson*

Elements of realistic model track include detail such as the joint bar, realistic rail and tie colors, and variations in ballast color. This is HO code 83 Walthers flextrack. *Jeff Wilson*

Mike Burgett models urban track with varying profiles with cork roadbed, using two layers for main track and one or none for other tracks. Shims ease track down to lower profile. Note the ballast color difference between the main and spur track. *Andy Sperandeo*

track (.055" tall, 80-pound rail). (For detailed information on modeling trackwork, see *Basic Trackwork for Model Railroaders*, Second Edition (Kalmbach, 2014.)

Most prototype track is jointed, with rail sections (typically 39 feet long, but lengths vary) bolted together at each end by joint bars, **2**. Variations include insulated joint bars, used to separate track sections into signal circuits—these are often painted yellow or orange—and compromise joint bars, which join rails of different sizes.

Steel tie plates keep the rails from biting into the ties, although some early track and secondary track (such as industrial spurs and some yard track) was laid without tie plates, **3**. Ties are generally wood, although concrete began increasing in popularity by the 1990s on many heavy main lines.

For good drainage, track should be elevated above surrounding ground. Roadbed is important for supporting the load of rolling stock and locomotives as well as for drainage. Crushed rock has long been the ideal choice, and is typically a layer at least 6" to 18" thick—and even taller on modern main lines.

However, on secondary lines, industrial spurs, and yards, ties are often directly on graded earth, sometimes on a bed of cinders (a readily available byproduct throughout the steam era). Even if some ballast was used, it often becomes hidden in weeds and brush, **4**.

Colors are important when modeling track. New treated ties are close to black; as they weather, they shift to shades of dark gray and brown, then light gray. Well-maintained main lines will have ties of consistent color, but the color of ties on urban secondary trackage usually varies greatly, **5**.

Note the ballast color in that photo: It appears gray, but in looking closely the color is not uniform, as individual stones vary widely in color. Beware of commercial ballast that is all the same color—it won't accurately capture the look of prototype track. Blending colors will result in better-looking track, **6**.

This low-profile switch stand is controlled manually, but has an electric lock to discourage tampering. *Gordon Odegard*

Three tracks of the Rock Island cross the four tracks of the Gulf, Mobile & Ohio and the Santa Fe on 12 diamonds at Joliet, Ill., in the 1950s. *Trains magazine collection*

Industrial track in cities gets complex: Here three turnouts are layered among each other, with two tracks tightly curving between buildings. The brick crossings, track in pavement at the dock, and weed-grown track (right) heading to other buildings are all modelable details. *Trains magazine collection*

Rail, likewise, varies in color from dark brown and black to lighter shades of brown and rust (reddish-orange). I like to paint rail sides with a brush or paint markers using a variety of these colors. The model photo also shows commercial joint bars (from Details West). These are easy to use and add greatly to realism. I use them wherever track is prominent in scenes, where viewers can easily spot them.

Varying track profiles can be modeled by altering the level of track—main tracks should be on taller roadbed, with spurs and secondary tracks with a lower profile, **7**.

Turnouts and special track

You'll often hear the terms "turnout" and "switch" used interchangeably, and you can usually do so without confusion (although on the prototype, "switch" refers to the moving parts, the points). The points move back and forth to guide trains on one of two routes (three for three-way turnouts). They can be powered by hand, **3**, or by electric or pneumatic machines. Powered turnouts are common on

main lines (controlled by dispatchers in Centralized Traffic Control areas) and within trackage controlled by interlocking towers.

On secondary track and spurs, manual control is common. Switch stands have large levers that are either rotated or lifted to move the switch rod back and forth, **8**. The switch stand or machine is on the headblock— extensions of the ties on either side of the switch rod. Turnouts on spurs connecting to a main line sometimes have electric locks on them.

High-level stands are typical on main tracks, with low-level stands on spurs. Faces on the stand have reflectors, and stands on busy tracks in yards and other areas were often illuminated by lanterns through the steam and early diesel eras.

Crossings, **9**, are found at junctions between lines or sometimes in industrial and yard tracks in tight areas. They're often called "diamonds" for their shape.

Because of the tight clearances and sharp curves often found in cities, urban trackwork—especially industrial lines and spurs—often has complex

assemblies of turnouts overlapping each other, along with curved crossings and turnouts, in tight areas, **10**.

Track bumpers are everywhere in cities and towns. They come in many shapes and sizes, from large single-piece bumpers to pairs of wheel stops to improvised bumpers like the wood ties in **4**.

Cities and towns are filled with abandoned trackwork. This can be old street trackage that was abandoned in place; spurs to industries that are no longer in business (or have switched to trucks); old interchange tracks; or lines that are no longer in service. Although modeling large areas of abandoned track takes valuable modeling space that could probably be better spent on active track, adding a couple of small areas of track that's obviously no longer in service can contribute to the atmosphere of a scene.

A variation on this is where track has been removed, but where it's obvious that it once was there. This could be indicated by an oddly shaped building or a patched-over area on a street where a track once crossed.

Bridges and elevated track

Street trackage and grade crossings are fascinating to model, but as vehicular traffic in cities increased, railroads looked for ways to avoid vehicular congestion. They did this by elevating or depressing track, both of which can provide interesting modeling possibilities. Bridges in urban areas can range from a single span crossing a street to an elevated viaduct that can carry track above surrounding streets for several blocks, **11**.

The style and type of bridges used in urban areas were dependent upon the era built, the length of the span, and the amount of clearance needed above or below. Into the early 1900s, through truss bridges were common where below-track clearance was required, **12**, or where spans exceeded the practical length of plate-girder designs; deck truss designs were used whenever below-bridge clearance wasn't an issue, **13**. By the early 1900s, plate-girder bridges (deck and through designs) became the default option.

Piers (middle supports) and abutments (end supports) of many designs carried bridges. Cut stone was common through the 1800s, with concrete or steel, **14**, after that. Abutments also act as retaining walls at the ends of a span, with wing walls to hold back neighboring fill.

New York Central's elevated West Side freight line in New York City eliminated more than 100 grade crossings. This is the view from about West 18th Street (foreground) to about West 26th Street. *New York Central*

Stone bridges can be found in many areas, especially along older lines in the Northeast, **15**. Many are more than 150 years old and still strong; their main challenge is restricted clearance where they cross roads and streets.

Long stretches of elevated track can be on a mix of fills and bridges, **16**. Fill is used wherever possible, and may be held back by retaining walls if needed. In dense urban areas, long bridges or viaducts are typical. Among the best known of these was New York Central's High Line in west Manhattan. First opened in

1933, the line traveled along 10th and 11th Avenues, eliminating more than 100 street crossings and cutting a tremendous amount of street congestion. Spurs and sidings were elevated, with the track passing directly through some structures, **11, 17**.

These elevated lines could be conventional bridge structures with plate-girder or truss spans atop block, concrete, or steel piers, but decorative concrete structures were built in some areas, **18**.

Elevated lines weren't only found in large cities. Many smaller cities also elevated track to ease congestion. Aurora, Ill., is one example, **19**. The Burlington's main line was elevated through town in 1922 on a series of concrete viaducts. Many of these examples illustrate that even though the rail line was elevated, the structures could still present hazards to vehicle traffic, with multiple posts and piers as well as low-clearance spans that don't clear modern trucks.

Elevated lines provide modeling possibilities, **20**. Keep an eye out for the details, including the surrounding city areas (see more on structures and details in Chapters 3 and 5).

Depressed track and tunnels

The other option for avoiding congestion is dropping the track below

This skewed through truss bridge at Easton, Pa., carried the Central of New Jersey over the Lehigh River and Third Street. Deck truss spans flank the through bridge. Note the concrete pier at left and the stone pier at right.
Historic American Engineering Record

At Parkersburg, W.Va., the Baltimore & Ohio crossed part of its approach to the Ohio River on a series of Warren deck truss spans supported by tapered cut stone piers. Farther east (out of view), plate girder spans were used. *William E. Barrett, Historic American Engineering Record*

The Illinois Terminal built its elevated line into St. Louis in the 1920s, using plate girder spans supported by steel posts. The railroad removed its overhead wire in 1958; this view is in October 1969. *Bob Trebing*

street level, **21**. This could be done for short stretches of main lines or industrial track or long stretches of main line. As an example, much of Amtrak's Northeast Corridor (former Pennsylvania and New Haven lines) is below grade, with street and pedestrian bridges carrying traffic above.

Wide cuts may have graded, grassy slopes on each side—common in open country and many suburban areas—but in metro areas where land is expensive, retaining walls are commonly used for both railroad and highway rights-of-way. Concrete became the most

This skewed stone arch bridge at Reading, Pa., was built in 1857 and still in service in this 1999 view. Although structurally sound, it's definitely not built for modern highway traffic. *Jet Lowe, Historic American Engineering Record*

Elevated track is often built on a combination of fill and bridges. This is the Rock Island's main line at Joliet, Ill., in the **1960s.** *J. David Ingles collection*

The New York elevated West Side line passed directly through some buildings. Some street trackage remained into the 1930s, as at the packing company branch houses at West 14th Street. *Trains magazine collection*

Some elevated trackage was ornate, as with these concrete pillars and spans on the Pennsylvania's elevated line along 25th Street in Philadelphia. *Joseph Elliott, Historic American Engineering Record*

common material for retaining walls by the early 1900s, **22**, but there are still plenty of cut stone retaining walls in place. Retaining walls can be decorative, but that is more common along roads and streets. Walls along railroads are most often plain; concrete walls may have a cap.

Retaining walls are built as low as possible to accomplish their job of holding back surrounding fill. This could mean a half-height wall with a graded hill behind it. Walls generally aren't built taller than the bridges that cross over rights-of-way, so any wall taller than 15 to 20 feet would be unusual. Multiple walls in terraced fashion can be found, with tracks, streets, and structures on two, three, or more levels,

23. Retaining walls in urban areas are often topped with fences or railings, especially if pedestrian areas or streets are along or near the edge.

Retaining walls can be great modeling tools, and there are many variations in walls, so look at prototype photos and examples for guidelines for placement, materials, and weathering.

In extreme cases, the railroad goes underground like a subway. For example, in New York City, New York Central's line to Grand Central Terminal headed into a tunnel at East 97th Street and Park Avenue, **24**. Because the underground track was extensive, the line was electrified (with outside third rail) to eliminate problems with exhaust gases from steam locomotives.

The Burlington elevated its main line through Aurora, Ill., in the 1920s. The spans and pillars are concrete. A westbound run-through train (with New York Central power) rolls on the line in the late 1960s. *Chicago, Burlington & Quincy*

That tunnel used a common modeling trick to hide track by having the tunnel entrance start under a highway. Conventional tunnel portals (stone or concrete) are also used to get tracks underground and through congested areas. An example is the Baltimore & Ohio's Howard Street Tunnel in Baltimore, **25**. The 1.4-mile tunnel (later extended) was originally electrified, but that was removed in the early 1950s with the coming of diesels.

Remember that cuts are cheaper than tunnels, so railroads will keep tracks open as far as possible before a tunnel entrance. Multi-track tunnels are significantly more expensive to build, so will only be used when traffic warrants.

Junctions

Junctions are where two or more rail lines cross or where one line branches off from another. This can be simple, as two single-track main lines crossing in a small town or city, or complex, with several multi-track lines crossing and branching to different routes, **26**. They are fascinating places, with complicated trackwork, multiple signals, a variety of control equipment, and lots of trains.

Junctions of rail lines are critical in large cities, enabling railroads to interchange cars. They're also vital for routing trains in many directions—

20

Doug Kirkpatrick captured the look of elevated track in an urban setting on his freelanced HO Virginian & Western layout. The background is a mix of structures and photos on the backdrop. *Paul J. Dolkos*

for example, between main lines and union passenger terminals, or transfer runs bringing cars from a yard of one railroad to that of another.

A downside for prototype railroads is that where two or more railroads—already with high traffic density, multiple tracks, and routes—meet at grade, the result can be delayed trains and slow operations. Junctions were mechanical headaches, with crossings and turnouts requiring extensive maintenance.

Keeping trains moving, and moving safely, is the main priority. Beginning in the late 1800s the common way to control busy junctions became

interlocking plants, where the levers that control the turnouts and signals are mechanically connected and interlocked to prevent conflicting routes from being selected. Their installation quickly became widespread; for example, Chicago by the 1910s had more than 130 interlocking plants.

Interlockings were usually controlled by two-story towers, with the operator and control levers in the upper story and the interlocking equipment below (although some installations were in single-story structures).

Among the most fascinating details of interlockings (and most appealing to modelers) is the signal system, **27**. For

21

Depressing lines below street level avoids congestion but can present clearance issues. These stone retaining walls are along the Reading in its namesake city, with the Walnut Street bridge overhead. *William E. Barrett, Historic American Engineering Record*

22

Concrete retaining walls became common by the early 1900s. This is on the former New York, New Haven & Hartford at New Haven, Conn., with a through truss bridge (built in 1907) carrying Olive Street over the four-track main line. *Historic American Engineering Record*

most of the 1900s these were typically semaphore signals, with searchlight and three-light signals becoming more common as towers were replaced by remote dispatcher control.

Interlockings are protected by distant and home signals. Distant signals, located away from the crossing, can be one- or two-head signals, and give advance notice that a train should reduce speed or approach the home signals preparing to stop. Home signals are at the junction itself. These are usually two- or three-head signals. The signal indications let train crews know whether they can proceed or have to stop, and for junctions with multiple route options, they also indicate the route that is aligned for the train.

Where traffic was light, manually controlled gates were common, **28**. These were common where two industrial branches—or perhaps a branch and secondary line—crossed.

The gate would be normally lined across one route, and trains from all directions would have to stop. Train crews themselves would move the gates.

Another option at less-busy junctions was an automatic interlocking. With these, signals were triggered by the first train to hit the approach track circuit. They were used on secondary lines or even main lines where the junction was a simple crossing—where no alternate routes were possible.

By the 1960s, railroads were simplifying junctions wherever possible, removing excess tracks and grade-separating some junctions. Interlocking towers had begun disappearing in favor of remote control by dispatchers. Many towers remained in service through the 1970s, but they are rare today. Even though the towers themselves have gone away, the junctions, traffic, and signals remain.

Of course, what's challenging for prototype railroads is fascinating for modelers, and junctions can be interesting visually as well as operationally. This can mean a simple crossing of two single-track lines with an interchange track in a small town, or a multi-track, multi-route collection of diamonds and turnouts in a large city.

Retaining walls allow multiple levels of tracks, streets, and structures in a shallow space. This 1950 view in Minneapolis shows the Soo Line *Mountaineer/Dominion* rolling near the Great Northern Station (lower tracks), next to the post office (top level) as it heads to the Milwaukee depot three blocks away. *Robert Milner*

A New York Central passenger train behind a class P-2 electric on third-rail power emerges from the tunnel at Park Avenue and East 97th Street in New York. The tunnel carries tracks underground to Grand Central Terminal. *Trains magazine collection*

The Baltimore & Ohio's Howard Street Tunnel carried traffic under Baltimore street traffic. The tunnel, originally 1.4 miles long, opened in 1895 and was electrified until the 1950s. *Historic American Engineering Record*

Water and fuel

Steam locomotives required frequent stops to add water and fuel. Water required replenishing more often, so a water tank would be located every 10 to 20 miles along most lines, **29**. All cities and many smaller towns would have them, usually near the depot so locomotives could take on water during station stops. In urban areas, tanks would also be located near yards (which often had full servicing facilities) or stations. Cities and yards were more likely to have a larger tank or tanks with multiple stand pipes.

Wood tanks were common through the steam era, with vertical staves surrounded by a series of steel bands. The spout was normally vertical. It was lowered to fill tenders. Tower bases could be wood or steel frames. Steel tanks could be found along some lines.

Coaling towers were not needed as frequently as water stops. They were primarily located at engine servicing terminals in cities (especially division points and crew-change stops), but some were found in intermediate towns or cities. Urban areas could have larger structures, sometimes with multi-track chutes under the structure itself. Although water and coal facilities were no longer needed after the demise of steam, some of the larger concrete coaling towers still stand, as tearing them down is expensive.

Diesels were far less needy. They are generally fueled at servicing terminals, but if they require fuel at other times it is a simple matter of having a fuel truck make a direct delivery, **30**. This was common in the early diesel era before railroads had established diesel fueling stations, and was also commonly done for switchers and other engines assigned to remote branches or yards.

Large-city engine terminals go beyond the scope of this book, but for more details and modeling ideas see Tony Koester's book *Steam & Diesel Locomotive Servicing Terminals* (Kalmbach, 2018).

Yards

Many cities feature rail yards, **31**. Including a yard on a layout is a matter of preference: They can provide a

You're aboard a Belt Railway of Chicago locomotive at Pullman Junction (Chicago). The BRC's tracks swing left to South Chicago; the Chicago & Western Indiana heads to the right. Note the double-slip switch in the foreground. *John Gruber*

These interlocking semaphore signals protect the approach tracks at Boston's South Station. The interlocking tower is between tracks in the distance.
William E. Barrett, Historic American Engineering Record

Light-traffic crossings were sometimes protected by manual gates. This is the Southern Pacific's Pasadena Branch crossing the Santa Fe line at Highland Park, Calif., in the late 1950s. *Donald Sims*

Water tanks (here with a separate standpipe, middle) and coal docks were located near many stations in small and large cities throughout the steam era. This wood tank and tower are on the Soo Line. *Gordon Odegard*

If a diesel couldn't make it back to a servicing facility, it was a simple matter of having a fuel truck stop by. This New York Central SW1 is getting a visit from a Sinclair truck at Troy, N.Y., in 1957. *Jim Shaughnessy*

great deal of visual and operational possibilities, but they take up a tremendous amount of space.

As Chapter 1 noted, yards (along with big engine facilities) were located in major cities on most railroads, with cities growing and spreading outward from these locations. Yards were typically adjacent to major manufacturing and industrial areas, making it easier to switch customers.

By the 1940s and 1950s, many businesses in these industrial areas were closing or moving to outlying areas. Railroads were looking to automate and expand yards to make them more efficient. Urban yards, hemmed in by surrounding buildings and streets, were not easily expanded or upgraded, so new yards were being built outside cities (where problems of vandalism and theft would be minimized, and security made easier).

For details on yard design and operations, with many photos and plans, see Andy Sperandeo's excellent book, *The Model Railroader's Guide to Freight Yards* (Kalmbach, 2004).

The Northern Pacific's Minneapolis yard was located adjacent to the city's milling district. Key details in this 1939 view include the industrial buildings and tracks in the background, with the partial retaining wall in front of them, and vehicles on the near-side street (again with retaining wall). *John Vachon, Library of Congress*

1

CHAPTER FIVE

Signs and details

Urban modeling offers myriad opportunities to use signs and other details. However, creating a realistic setting involves more than just placing random details into a scene. Detailing must be done in a prototypical fashion, with thought to what's appropriate for specific cities and regions, along with the proper eras for the signs and details being used, **1**.

This busy HO street scene includes structure signs from various sources, a free-standing gas station sign, and details including highway signs, mailbox, phone booth, stoplight, streetlights, parking meters, soda machine, figures, and vehicles. *Jeff Wilson*

This lamppost in New York City carries several signs in 1938, including street name, one-way, route marker, and no parking. There's also a mailbox and, at the bottom, wire trash basket. *Walker Evans, Library of Congress*

An otherwise beautifully detailed circa-1940s Midwestern streetcar scene will be spoiled by inclusion of a red stop sign at a street corner. Likewise, a 1995-era city scene with a prominent billboard advertising a new 1961 Chevy will not be realistic, no matter how high the level of detail. However, having a model of a 1961 Chevy in that scene could work—as long as most of the other vehicles are from the 1980s and '90s.

If you model a specific prototype and time period, getting these details correct becomes easier. Check prototype photos, books, and other sources to see what was actually being used. If you freelance, it's especially important that these details be used in a realistic manner: Base your choices on prototype scenes and railroads from the region and era you've chosen.

Signs

Signs are a great way to indicate the era and location of a layout. Signs and their artwork are eye-catching, and urban modeling provides many opportunities for modeling many types: street signs, storefront signs, hanging signs, industrial signs, billboards (free-standing and those painted directly on buildings) and other advertisements, rooftop signs, and others.

And for modelers, the internet and wide availability of photo-manipulation software have made modeling all of these signs easier than ever before. Together with commercially available signs, there really is no reason for not accurately modeling these important details.

Street signs

Stroll down a city street or look at a period photo of a street scene and among the first thing that jumps out is the sheer number of street and traffic signs, 2: stop signs, highway route numbers, street names, directional arrows and one-way signs, bus stop signs, parking information signs, speed limit signs, and warning signs for curves, signals, pedestrians, passing zones, schools, and (of course) railroad crossings.

Early traffic signs weren't consistent in design, size, colors, or usage. The first stop sign didn't even appear until 1915 (although the first electric traffic

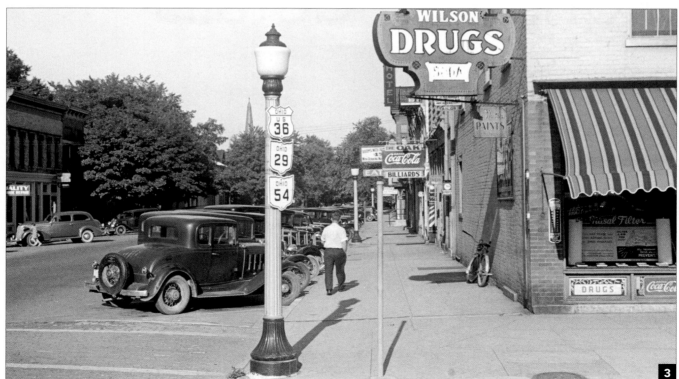

This ornamental lamppost in Urbana, Ohio, carries cut-out U.S. and Ohio route markers in 1938. Structures have a variety of hanging signs. *Ben Shahn, Library of Congress*

signals appeared in 1912)—the increase in automobile traffic (and vehicle speeds) were making early streets and intersections dangerous places for vehicles and pedestrians alike.

Cities and counties began putting up their own signs to try to regulate traffic, but by World War I a move toward uniform signs and markings had begun. Several states adopted uniform standards by the early 1920s, with the first national guidelines published in 1925 (albeit separate guidelines for rural and urban use).

Among these guidelines were standard shapes for signs including the now-familiar round for railroad crossing warning signs, octagonal stop signs, and diamond shapes for caution signs, all with yellow as a background color. This also marked the official adaptation of red, green, and yellow for signal lights, which had already been in use since the 1910s.

The best guide for appropriate practices and sign designs for a given period is the *Manual on Uniform Traffic Control Devices*, or MUTCD. They are issued periodically by the U.S. Government, and most states follow them. You can find copies of the current edition, as well as many old editions (and predecessor-group guidelines) dating back to the 1920s at trafficsign.us/oldmutcd.html.

Non-control signs (street name signs, bus stop signs, parking signs, etc.) came in many shapes, colors, sizes, and styles, and were often unique to a locale. They can be a distinctive feature that identifies a particular city and era.

Highway route numbers can positively identify a city (and even a specific intersection). Numbered roadways for the U.S. highway system were adopted in 1926. These signs were a distinctive cutout shield design, and lettering included the state in a top section with "U.S." above the number in the lower part of the sign, **3**. In 1961 this was simplified to a square sign with black border and white shield with just the route number. Many of the older-style signs remained in place for several years, and a few could be found through the 1970s in some areas.

Interstate highway signs, which

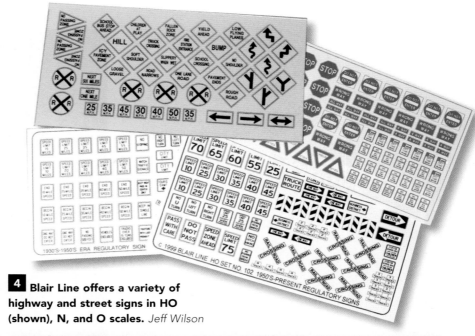

4 **Blair Line offers a variety of highway and street signs in HO (shown), N, and O scales.** *Jeff Wilson*

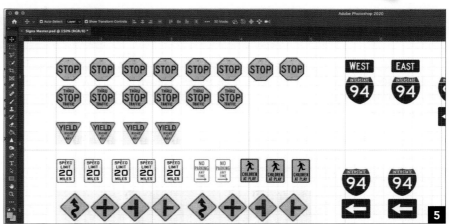

I made this group of signs in Photoshop using a combination of photos of real signs and sign artwork from old driver's training manuals. They were cleaned up and resized. *Jeff Wilson*

The watchman is flagging the crossing with a stop sign after lowering the manually controlled gates at this Reading crossing in Philadelphia in 1948. *Leslie R. Ross*

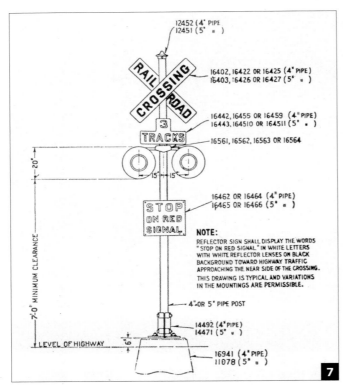

By the 1940s, the Association of American Railroads had refined recommendations for signs and signals for railroad crossings. *AAR*

The familiar round crossing warning signs initially had stripes in a + pattern; by the 1940s the stripes were x-pattern. *Library of Congress*

Wig-wag signals were popular from the 1910s to the 1960s and came in many styles. This one is on the Santa Fe at Hermosa Beach, Calif., in 1960. *Donald Sims*

first appeared in 1956 with initial construction of the system's roadways, have a different shield style and are blue and red with white lettering. It's rare that an interstate highway is featured on a model railroad, but these signs can often be found on urban streets as directional signs (as in "to Interstate 94") with arrow signs at intersections.

State highway (route) signs follow their own unique designs, which have also evolved over the years. Many feature outlines of the states or other distinctive shapes. County markers likewise follow different designs, many of which include the county name.

Sign designs and lettering styles have changed over time. Probably the most notable is the venerable stop sign, which until 1954 was yellow with black lettering. Reflective beads were often used on these and other signs to increase visibility at night. In 1954, red was adopted as the sign color, with white lettering. These were quickly updated on major routes, but some small-town and rural areas still had yellow stop signs well into the 1960s.

The crossbuck with paired flashing lights was the most common automatic warning device from the 1930s through the rest of the century. Lettering varied; this one is in Vermont in 1939. *Russell Lee, Library of Congress*

Griswold signals were common in the Midwest. These had a stop sign that rotated when a train approached. Extra pairs of flashers are used where additional streets approach the crossing. *J. David Ingles*

The triangular yield sign was introduced in 1954, and was initially yellow with black lettering. In 1971, this changed to white with a heavy red border and red lettering, although again many older signs remained in place after that date.

Lettering styles have changed significantly in all types of signs as well. This is well illustrated by looking at speed limit signs through the eras. Lettering has shifted from a more-angular font to a curved style.

Several model manufacturers offer road and street signs, notably Blair Line, **4**, which has several HO, N, and O scale sets covering many eras, and Microscale, which offers sign decals. You can also make your own by scanning photos or artwork or taking digital photos and printing them out, **5**. The technique is the same as described in making building flats in Chapter 3. Resize them as needed so they print out at the correct sizes.

Successfully modeling these details is far more than simply cutting out

By the 1960s, busy automatic crossings typically had gates and overhead flashing lights. This is on the Illinois Central at Lockport, Ill., in the late 1970s. *Library of Congress*

Whistle posts come in many styles; from left: Pennsylvania Keystone; wood post; Southern Ry. whistle notation; and modern "no whistle" sign. *Wood sign: B.A. Bentz; others: Robert S. McGonigal*

Mileposts typically feature simple numbers on a white sign on a post; some, like this one, were mounted on line poles. The pole survives, with the top cut off (and other line poles removed). *Library of Congress*

Styles of speed limit signs varied by railroad. This Burlington Northern sign includes speeds for talgo (T), passenger (P), and freight (F) trains. *Robert S. McGonigal*

Common signs in and near cities are yard limit and yard limit and station approach signs. The short sign in the second photo is a flanger post. *All: Gordon Odegard*

signs and planting them along the street. Make sure you install them in a realistic manner: Follow prototype photos and MUTCD guidelines if you have any doubts.

Light and signal poles are often used for mounting street signs, and others are free-standing. Early signposts were often wood, and wood is still used in many areas. Steel posts became common, featuring either round pipes or U-shaped channel with bolt (mounting) holes along the channel. You can model wood posts with stripwood stained a dark gray with brown highlights (new posts) or a lighter weathered gray (old posts). For steel posts, use styrene rod or brass or steel wire painted black or dark gray.

Crossing signs

Urban grade crossings between railroads and streets are focal points of many layouts. Heavy auto traffic and frequent train movements made such crossings dangerous places, and they were either passive—protected only by signs—or active, with gates, bells, flashing lights, and perhaps a crossing guard with a sign or controlling gates, **6**.

The basic protective sign is the crossbuck, the familiar X-shaped sign with "Rail Road Crossing" lettering, **7**. Although today these are standardized with sign boards at a 90-degree angle, many railroads originally opted for signs at a shallower (50- or 60-degree) angle.

Through the 1920s, many installations had signs of varying designs and lettering. "Watch out for the cars" and "Watch out for the engine" were common alternates. Some of these alternate signs lasted into the 1960s.

Glass bead reflectors were common on the lettering of these signs through the 1940s, until the advent of Scotchlite and other reflective surfaces. Posts of crossbucks were often striped to attract attention. Additional signs include the number of tracks, and some railroads added signs indicating the railroad name. Since the 2000s, signs at grade crossings include identification numbers to allow contacting authorities in emergencies.

The familiar round yellow warning signs first appeared in the 1920s, and are mounted in advance of grade crossings—usually at least 500 feet, but sometimes closer in urban areas. These initially had the crossing as a vertical/horizontal +, **8**; since the 1940s they have had the now-standard X pattern.

Busy crossings in metro areas were often guarded by watchmen in elevated towers, with manually operated gates. These fascinating installations, common through the 1940s, are discussed in Chapter 3.

It wasn't practical to have a flagman guard every crossing, so railroads moved early to provide automatic protection at some crossings. The first such device was a bell, mounted on the crossing sign and triggered by an electrical circuit in the rails. Although reasonably effective for pedestrians and horse-drawn wagons, they weren't good at attracting attention of drivers in then-noisy automobiles.

Wig-wag signals first appeared around 1910, adding motion and light to warn motorists, **9**. These have a red light mounted on a mast that swings back and forth, imitating the motion of a flagman swinging a lantern (a popular prototype was the Magnetic Flagman, the trade name for signals made by the Magnetic Signal Co.).

These grew in popularity through the 1930s, and could be found in many designs. On some the arm hung downward; others had the arm projecting upward. Some were

Commercial signs include these paper business signs from City Classics, billboards from JL Innovative Design, decal logos from Microscale, and plastic-backed store signs from Blair Line. *Jeff Wilson*

Many items can be scanned for making your own digital signs, including matchbooks, road maps, and product labels. *Jeff Wilson*

Hanging signs—many with custom-shaped neon tubes—were common in cities and towns through the 1960s, and some are still in use. This bank sign is in Carlyle, Ill. *John Margolies; Library of Congress*

mounted on arms extending outward from posts; others were centered on brackets on a pole. Many were installed before crossbucks became standard, but most of these early wig-wags eventually had crossbucks added—either to the wig-wag's pole or on a separate post next to the signal.

They were usually installed next to the street or road, but some were prominently mounted on pedestals or bases in the middle of a street—better to attract motorists' attention.

By the 1930s and '40s the trend moved toward automatic flashing signals and gates, but some wig-wags remained in service—especially on branch lines and industrial areas—into the 2000s.

Flashing light signals were first installed in 1913 (in New Jersey). Photo **10** shows an Association of American Railroads standard design from 1939; the basic design has remained similar ever since, with key changes being larger lenses (from 8" lenses on 20" targets, to 12" lenses in the 1970s, to 24" targets in the 1980s. Variations include multiple sets of flashers directed at side streets, **11**, and overhead on arms.

Automatic arms began appearing with flashers on high-traffic crossings in the 1920s, and these became common from World War II onward. These were typically black-and-white striped through the 1960s, and red-

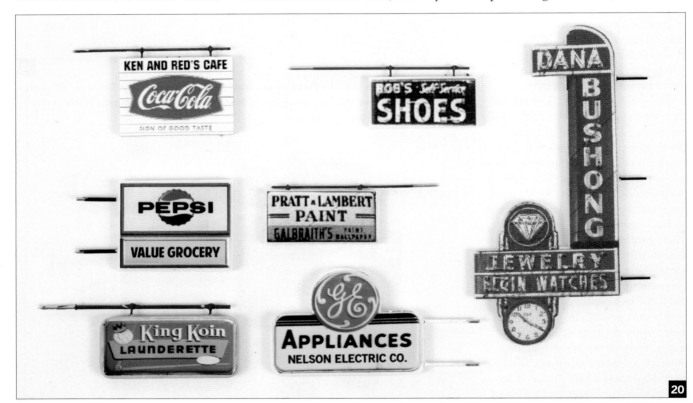

These HO scale hanging and projecting signs were made by photographing real signs or scanning logos and printing them out, some with additional lettering. The shoe store and paint signs are from Blair Line. *Jeff Wilson*

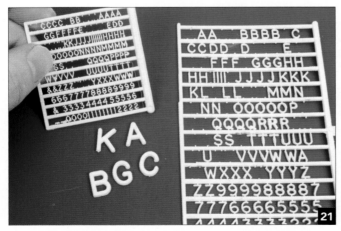

Slaters makes three-dimensional plastic lettering as small as **2mm tall.** *Jeff Wilson*

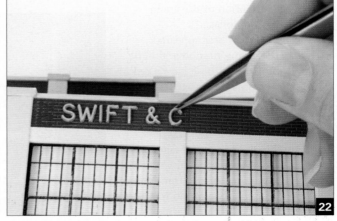

Raised lettering can be used directly on buildings, on rooftop signs, or on billboards. *Jeff Wilson*

and-white striped since then, **12**.

Automatic installations became the norm by the late 1930s. A 1935 *Railway Age* article noted that as of that year, 17,000 of the United States' 205,000 grade crossings had been equipped with automatic warning devices (flashers or wig-wags), but about 6,200 were still protected by watchmen (about three-quarters of those with gates). Of those, 1,200 were manned full-time and 5,000 were part time.

For modeling, NJ International offers a variety of operating crossing signals including period and modern flashers with crossbucks (including a Griswold version) and gates. Busch, Tomar, and Walthers have also offered crossing signals.

Right-of-way signs

You'll find a variety of signs along railroad rights-of-way, and especially in cities and towns. Whistle posts are placed in advance of grade crossings, indicating where trains should sound horns or whistles. Modern signs usually feature a simple W on a small square white sign on a post, but older signs varied widely in style by railroad, **13**. Pennsylvania's distinctive keystone design left no doubt as to the railroad line you were viewing. Other variations included tall, white wooden posts, an X instead of W, or the Southern Railway's sign that showed the whistle pattern. Yet another variation was a bell post (usually "R" for "ring"), often found near stations.

A modern variation, starting in the late 20th century, is the no-whistle sign, used by some railroads where cities and towns have enacted ordinances prohibiting or restricting horns and whistles.

Mileposts mark the distance from the line's originating point. They can be free-standing signs or fastened to a neighboring line pole, **14**. As with whistle posts, early signs could very in styles among railroads.

Speed-limit signs may feature a single number, or have separate numbers for freight and passenger trains, **15**. They are commonly found in and near large urban areas, where train speed limits typically drop.

Painted signs with dry transfer masks

You can use dry transfer lettering and designs to make painted-on signs in any scale. The advantage of this technique is that it eliminates decal film and dry transfer material, leaving only paint on the model surface.

Start by painting the panel the lettering color (usually white). Add dry transfers, **1**, burnishing the transfer sheet with medium pressure: You want the film to transfer and hold to the surface, but not be firmly attached. The photos show a Clover House set intended for a refrigerator car; you can use individual lettering as well.

Next, paint the background color. An airbrush provides the best results, but a spray can will also work. The key is to use several very light coats, taking care to spray perpendicular to the surface to minimize chances of paint bleeding under the dry transfers. Too heavy a coat will also effectively glue the transfers in place, making them impossible to remove cleanly.

Once the paint is thoroughly dry (wait a day or two), press masking tape or gaffer tape to the area, rubbing it firmly to the surface. Peel the tape up, and the dry transfers should come up with the tape, revealing the lettering color beneath them, **2**. You may have to use additional pieces of tape.

You'll probably have to touch up some areas with a fine brush, or use a hobby knife to remove stubborn bits of transfer film.

Weather the sign as desired to create the effect you're looking for—chalks and thinned oversprays of the brick color work well for aging.

This sign looks painted on because it is. It's receiving a weathering coat of brick-colored powdered chalk to make it appear old. *Jeff Wilson photos*

Paint the background white, then burnish the dry transfers in place, using just enough pressure to transfer the lettering.

Paint the area black. When it dries, press masking or gaffer tape over the lettering and peel it up to reveal the painted lettering.

Yard limit signs, **16**, mark the point where speed and train rights restrictions begin (many urban industrial areas and branches are all operated under yard limits rules). You'll also find approach signs (usually at one mile) for yard limits, junctions, and stations. These were in several shapes and designs;

angles and triangles were common.

Flanger posts alert plow crews to lift flanger blades (which plow snow from between the rails) in advance of grade crossings and other between-rail obstructions. They're usually small black flags at angles mounted at the top of a signpost.

Signs painted directly on buildings were common from the late 1800s through the mid-1900s. Black backgrounds with white lettering and borders were most common.
Library of Congress

Other signs include no trespassing, no dumping, clearance signs of various types (especially at bridges and where buildings and platforms are next to tracks), and signs indicating the beginning and end of track signal circuits.

Modeling these is easy with commercial signs from Blair Line and others. You can also make your own as shown earlier with street signs.

Storefront, hanging, and free-standing business signs

Storefront and business-name signs can accomplish many things. Specific signs taken from prototype buildings can set a modeled scene in a specific location and time. They can provide a general feel or mood for a city or region by using familiar product, chain store, or business names and logos. And they can also be used for fun to immortalize friends and relatives with their names.

Many model kit and ready-built structures include signs, either decals or paper prints. If the signs reflect a real business, feel free to use them; otherwise, I recommend discarding the manufacturers' fake signs and coming up with your own.

To keep a realistic feel, do some research to know when particular businesses came into being and disappeared, and when their various logos were changed and updated. For example, if you have a corner gas station in the Midwest, branding it for Skelly works well if you're modeling 1970, but not for 1990, since the company was bought out in 1977.

However, some older signs remained in place long after companies went out of business (or after logos changed). This was more common in small towns and run-down urban areas—businesses are usually quick to keep things updated in busy areas.

There are many sources for modeling these signs. Microscale has many decal sets that include signs and common manufacturer and product logos covering many eras. Other decal and dry-transfer signs and alphabet sets are made by Woodland Scenics,

Clover House, and others. Paper signs are made by Blair Line, JL Innovative Design, and others, **17**.

Keep an eye out for any materials that have the company name and logo you're looking for, such as old advertisements, matchbooks, stationery, promotional materials, and packaging, **18**. Scan the internet as well. You can scan materials or download digital files to resize and make your own signs using photo-editing software. (You can use these materials, including trademarked logos and designs, to make signs for your own use; you do not generally have the right to distribute them to others.)

Hanging signs on storefront buildings were quite common through the 1960s, **19**, and their color and variety can make for fascinating modeled street scenes. Although they're becoming rare, they can still be found. Many feature national product logos with the store name added. Others featured neon lights; many such signs remained in place long after the neon tubes had long since disappeared.

These can be modeled easily by gluing the graphics to a piece of styrene, then mounting it on a length of brass wire or piano wire extending from the structure, **20**. Again, try to keep the signs appropriate for the era. The Library of Congress has a number of these from the John Margolies collection and other sources that will work as starting points for models; you can also use common logos and add

After this Occident Flour sign was painted, it was obscured by an adjacent building. When that building was torn down in the 1990s, the old sign was revealed. *Jeff Wilson*

I scanned the sign from 24, straightened it in Photoshop, printed it on white decal paper, and applied it to a storefront HO structure. *Jeff Wilson*

lettering to customize a sign for a local business.

Free-standing signs were typically found in front of gas stations, restaurants, and other stores that were set back from the street. Logos can be fastened to styrene, with a post made of brass or styrene tubing or channel. The Mileage gas sign in **1** was scanned from a road map, mounted on styrene, and glued to a pole from a Walthers gas station kit.

Separate three-dimensional lettering can be found on industrial buildings and storefronts alike. Plastic signboard (or directory sign) letters are widely available in sizes from ½" and larger. Another option is three-dimensional lettering designed as stick-on graphics, sold in craft stores and online in a variety of styles. Injection-molded letters as small as 2mm are made by Slaters (slatersplastikard.com), **21**. These can be applied directly to a structure, **22**, or to a free-standing, hanging, or rooftop sign.

Billboards are common in urban areas. They can advertise local businesses or national or local products. Note the advertising company name above the boards on these circa-1940 Minneapolis signs. *Library of Congress*

Early electric lampposts were often decorative or ornate, and many had multiple light globes. Other details in this circa-1940 scene in Rock Rapids, Iowa, include a corner mailbox, awnings, and curb ramps. *Jeff Wilson collection*

28

Through the early 1900s, many smaller towns had lights mounted above streets on cross wires instead of lights on poles. This is Centralia, Kan., in 1938.

John Vachon, Library of Congress

Painted signs

Signs painted directly on buildings were and are common in industrial areas and on retail buildings, **23**. They can be advertisements, but the most common style features the company name in white lettering on a black background. These sign panels usually extend the entire length of the building, or between definite hard borders (such as pilasters), with lettering extending the full width of the panel.

These can be re-created in a couple of ways. The simplest is to paint a black background area and add individual decal or dry transfer lettering. You can also use dry transfers as a mask for painting to create signs that are actually painted in place. See the sidebar on page 67.

Product billboards were commonly painted directly on buildings in cities from the late 1800s onward. This could be on tall buildings, or at sidewalk level on otherwise blank walls. Ads for beverages, candy, food products, and tobacco were common. Many of these signs lasted long after their products were no longer produced (or prices

changed—Coca-Cola can no longer be had for a nickel a bottle, despite what a faded sign in my hometown still promised into the 2000s).

Signs long out of date should be appropriately weathered, although some old signs survived in much better shape by being covered up by new neighboring buildings, which years later were demolished, revealing the sign—the Occident Flour sign in **24** is an example.

Decals work well for these types of signs, **25**, allowing the graphics to assume the texture of the surface (usually brick). You can use paper signs as well. The time-honored technique for paper signs is to sand the back, making them as thin as possible. Spread white glue or matte medium on the back and apply it, using a fingernail or toothpick to firmly press the sign into the brick pattern of the surface. They can be weathered as needed.

Billboards

Billboards are large signs that can be free standing, usually framed on multiple posts, **26**, although modern billboards are often on large single posts.

Billboards could also be framed and attached to structures or mounted near the edges of rooftops, both common in urban areas. These are similar to the painted-on signs described earlier, but billboard graphics are generally not meant to be permanent, and are changed on a regular basis.

You can set the date of your layout with billboards. For example, a billboard for a 1956 Chevrolet doesn't leave much doubt about the period being modeled. Almost any product or company can be the subject, with automobiles, beverages, food products, restaurants, and stores being popular subjects.

A wide variety of billboard kits and artwork is made by Bar Mills, Blair Line, BLMA, City Classics, JL Innovative Design, Microscale, Miller Engineering, Scenic Express, Woodland Scenics, and others. Billboards graphics also relatively easy to make combining various graphics and lettering in the same manner as structure signs. As with building signs, these can be output as either paper or decals.

A variation on standard billboards is three-dimensional or shaped signs with separate lettering, cutouts, or other effects. Kits for this type of sign are available from Bar Mills, Blair Line, Miller Engineering, Scenic Express, and Woodland Scenics.

Streetlights

Baltimore was the first major U.S. city to install gas lights as streetlights, in 1816. Other major cities soon followed. Electric lights followed, with many arc light installations by the 1890s, with incandescent lamps following by the turn of the century.

Early streetlights were relatively dim, so they often featured multiple light globes mounted on each pole, **27**, while others had single fixtures. These typically had cast-iron posts, with ornate fluting and trim on the posts. Many had lantern-style enclosures, mimicking the designs of the earlier gas lights. Hanging lights above streets, **28**, could also be found, especially in smaller towns.

By the 1920s and '30s, streetlights were getting taller, with pole-mounted lights on arms extending out from the

This ornate overhead streetlight is at the corner of East 61st Street and First Avenue in New York City in 1938.
Library of Congress

pole, **29**. Ornate fixtures again were typical, with fluted metal poles and decorative trim on arms through the art-deco era.

By the 1950s, practicality was outweighing ornamentation, and most new installations featured what have come to be known as boulevard-style lights, with fixtures at the end of arms, **30**, on simple metal tubular poles (or often on existing wood utility poles). These followed similar designs but varied in detail (General Electric and Westinghouse were the major manufacturers, and each offered multiple models that evolved over the years).

Mercury-vapor lights began replacing incandescent lights in the late 1940s, followed by high-pressure sodium fixtures in the 1970s. Today, most new installations feature light-emitting diodes (LEDs).

The important thing for modelers is the appearance. Older-style lights lasted longer in some cities and towns than others, and some cities have installed classic-style ornate lamps in urban-renovation areas. Use prototype photos as a guide for what would be

appropriate for what you model.

In modeling, you have two choices: working and non-working models, **31**. Models are available from Brawa, Miniatronics, Walthers, Woodland Scenics, and others. If you like to operate your layout at night, or want to try night photography, working streetlights add a very realistic mood and feel. They do add extra expense and are more work to install.

Stoplights

Busy city intersections were controlled by traffic control officers as needed into the 1910s. The first traffic-control signals were manually controlled, consisting of signs facing each traffic direction, which could be rotated (usually by a traffic cop), **32**.

Traffic-control signals—commonly known as stoplights—began appearing in the 1910s, with the first installation in 1914. Early signals used red and green lights—colors adopted from typical railroad signals. Through the rest of the teens, signals were controlled by officers at the intersection.

Automatic lights were first used in

Starting in the 1950s, streetlights in most areas became simpler in design, with plain poles and curved arms with fixtures at the ends. *Library of Congress*

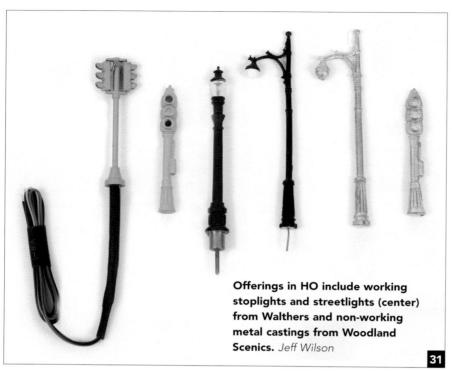

Offerings in HO include working stoplights and streetlights (center) from Walthers and non-working metal castings from Woodland Scenics. *Jeff Wilson*

31

1920, in Los Angeles, with red and green lights and semaphore arms, **33**. A bell would ring as the signals changed and semaphores retracted and came out for each direction. The semaphores proved to be difficult to see in traffic and at night, so future signals used lights only, although many of these semaphore signals lasted into the 1940s.

Installations varied by the amount of traffic and the arrangement of the intersection. Some early installations had a single four-faced signal, usually suspended on a cable above the intersection. By the late 1930s, most areas required at least two signals facing in each direction. This could be a combination of pole-mounted or hanging signals.

Signal styles varied widely among manufacturers. Ornate posts and fittings were common early. Another variation was "stop" and "go" lettering

32

The first traffic control devices were manually controlled signs, like this one with "STOP" and "GO" that was rotated by an officer. This is in the 1910s in Washington, D.C. *Library of Congress*

The first automatic stoplights were installed in Los Angeles in 1920. They had red/green lights and semaphores that extended with the signals (the GO and STOP arms are changing in this view). *Library of Congress*

on the red and green lenses, **34**, a practice banned by the late 1940s. Signal design evolved to larger lenses, going from an 8"-diameter to 12" diameter by the 1960s, initially for just the red lens, then for all lenses.

By the 1950s, turn arrows, crosswalk indicators, and other extras were becoming common at busy intersections. Where signals often were only pole-mounted on corners, new installations often had overhead signals on arms for better visibility. The styles of these evolved, becoming simpler and more plain over the years, but older, more ornate signals sometimes remained in service in older neighborhoods and low-traffic areas. Check prototype photos for your era and area to see appropriate.

Modelers in HO have the option of working three-light signals from Walthers, or non-operating signals from Walthers, Woodland Scenics, and others. Options in N scale are more limited, but Busch once offered operating signals, and several non-branded models can be found on eBay and other online sources.

Utility poles and lines

Utility poles and their corresponding electrical and communication lines were prominent features in urban areas from the late 1800s onward, **35**. As municipal power plants increased in number and size, the power requirements of large cities often led to busy poles with dozens of wires, creating a fascinating (but hazardous and difficult to model) effect—you can see this in several photos in Chapters 1, 3, and 4.

As their complexity and number grew in the 1900s, most cities reorganized and simplified wiring, moving to underground service for utilities whenever possible. The number of pole lines and wires dropped significantly, but streets still often had busy pole lines.

Urban utility poles can carry electric lines, telephone lines, and—since the 1960s—cable television lines. We'll keep our discussion to distribution lines—those that directly feed businesses and residences.

Electric lines are at the top. The number of wires depends upon the

Some early stoplights had lettering on the lenses, as on this four-sided, post-mounted signal in Hartford, Conn., in 1941. *Marion Post Wolcott*

Overhead lines trace many paths in this 1941 view of Little Falls, N.Y. Electric lines are at the top of poles, with various communication lines below. Also note the design of the stoplights. *John Collier, Library of Congress*

number of circuits carried. Transformers step down the power, with wires then running to individual buildings. Most users will receive single-phase AC, so only one transformer is used; larger businesses and industrial companies (those using heavy machinery) require three-phase AC, so you'll see three transformers at the step-down locations for those customers. Electric lines should be at least 27 feet above rail lines and 22 feet above highways.

Lower on the pole (with at least 40" of clearance below electric lines) will be telephone lines. These can be on crossarms similar to railroad communication lines, with 4- to 10-pin arms common. Since the 1960s, bundled lines and heavier cables have been the norm for phone and other non-electric utilities, with a single heavy black cable hung on a steel line.

Railroads have their own separate communication lines. These pole lines follow the right-of-way whenever possible, and don't share poles with public utility lines. By the early 1900s,

the majority of railroad lines had one or more 10-pin crossarms (five insulators on each side of the pole). Branch and secondary lines might only have a single arm using a few wires; main lines could have two, three, or more arms with wires on almost every position.

As railroads moved to radio communication in the 1960s and began eliminating many stations, the number of wires dropped, then pole lines began disappearing completely. With the move to track-based signal systems, pole lines are rare today.

Modelers in HO have several options to re-create these details, **36**. Among the best are the HO electric utility poles from Walthers (set 933-3101 includes multiple styles of crossarms and transformers) and Rix telegraph poles, which are accurate models of common railroad poles with 10-pin crossarms. Also, Rapido makes prestrung railroad poles and lines.

Modeling the wires themselves is more challenging, and not all modelers choose to add them. If done well, they

can add a great deal of interest and realism; however, if done poorly they can detract from a scene. They can also attract dust and get in the way of operations and maintenance.

My favorite material for lines is Berkshire Junction's EZ Line, an elastic thread. In HO, the fine material works well for phone and telegraph wires, and the heavy for electric lines, **37**. Some modelers have had good luck with monofilament or fine thread.

Sidewalk details

Town and city sidewalks are busy places. On the sidewalks themselves, you'll find ventilation grates, doors covering freight elevators, coal chutes for neighboring buildings, and manholes and covers for various systems.

Mailboxes are typically located at intersections or key traffic points in metro areas, **2, 27**. The familiar, common style is a metal box with rounded top, pull-down horizontal door, and four feet. You'll also find many smaller versions mounted to posts (sometimes to utility poles or lampposts). These were painted olive drab until 1955, but as of July 4 of that year, they began being painted red and blue with white lettering. This was again modified in 1971 to dark blue.

Fire hydrants are located at regular intervals along streets. These are traditionally painted red, but can be found in many other colors—many cities key the colors to their water-flow capacity.

Phone booths are often found along city streets. Pay phones and booths were originally indoor locations, with the first outdoor wooden booths appearing in 1905. Metal-framed glass booths (often with signs on top) began appearing in the 1950s. By the 1970s, enclosed booths were being replaced by smaller, simpler devices—usually a phone mounted on a post with a hood covering it. Public outdoor phones can still be found, but became rare by the 2000s.

Newsstands have been staples of city areas since the 1800s. Some are actually storefront buildings, but many are stand-alone structures on sidewalks, **38**. These range from small carts and portable stands moved by their owners to larger, semi-permanent structures. Along with stacks of newspapers and rows of colorful magazines on shelves, these also often sell items such as candy, cigarettes, and cigars.

Many other details can be found along streets and sidewalks, including vending machines, parking meters, fences, pedestrian benches, trash cans, and junk and debris of many types. Stores often place products outside their doors along sidewalks in nice weather.

Walthers, Woodland Scenics, JL Innovative Design, Bar Mills, and many others offer a tremendous variety of detail items that can be used in model scenes, **1**. Be sure to use these details in logical places and arrangements. As all of these details have evolved over time, they can be important in setting the era of a layout.

Figures

Towns and cities are centers of activity, and even a small city or town scene can absorb hundreds of miniature figures.

This HO scene includes a Walthers utility pole, crossarms, and transformer with a lower Rix crossarm for communication lines. The lines are EZ Line, with thread for the heaviest line heading for a building at right. *Jeff Wilson*

Painted figures have been available in a tremendous variety of poses from Bachmann, Busch, BTS, Herpa, Kibri, LaBelle, Merten, Noch, Preiser, Walthers, and Woodland Scenics.

You can save a great deal of money by painting your own figures. Sets of unpainted figures are offered by Preiser and Walthers, among others. You can use any common craft or modeling paints on figures—just use a fine-point brush, flat-finish paints, and take your time. Looking at color photos from the era you model is a good way to select proper clothing colors.

When arranging figures, make sure they are in logical places, poses, and groupings: two or three people talking to each other on a sidewalk, several passengers waiting on a station platform, or a worker reaching for a crate on a factory loading dock.

Save the best and most-detailed (best-painted) figures for foreground

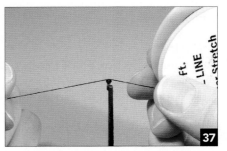

Berkshire Junction's elastic EZ Line works well for utility lines. Place a dab of super glue atop an insulator, then hold the line in place until the glue takes hold. *Jeff Wilson*

scenes and where figures stand on their own. Less-detailed figures can go into crowds and be placed on side streets and background scenes. Figures inside buildings but visible in windows and doorways also needn't be detailed—just the impression that they're there is sufficient to give structures life.

You can also "edit" figures into

Newsstands are common on city streets, ranging from small portable stands like this to larger structures. This is Chicago in the 1940s. *Library of Congress*

different poses—for example, removing one or both arms and repositioning them to better suit their intended location. This also helps hide the heritage of some of the more-common figures' poses.

Vehicles

Autos and trucks play a vital role in placing your layout in a specific era. Business names on trucks can identify a region or specific city; license plates can imply the state modeled (go to acme.com/licensemaker and have some fun!). The number of vehicles helps show how busy an area is, and the type of vehicles in industrial areas help tell the story of the products being made or handled.

Figures can be placed in many vehicles to give them a reason for being in traffic, conferring the appearance of cars and trucks on their way to places as opposed to a bunch of driverless cars that have for some reason been abandoned in the middle of the street.

Another easy modification is to turn the front wheels on some vehicles, **39**. This makes turning vehicles appear

Vehicle appearance can be much approved by adding figures to driver's seats and by turning the front wheels of some cars. This is an HO scale Classic Metal Works Dodge. *Jeff Wilson*

much more realistic.

Most of us have a variety of vehicle models we've acquired over the years, and some are no doubt better than others. As with figures, keep your best, most-realistic cars and trucks in the foreground or where they can stand alone. Those older, less-detailed models can work well in distant scenes, on side streets or in large groups (such as parking lots).

Make sure that, as with figures, your

vehicle groupings are realistic. Cars waiting at a stop sign or red light, for example, can be placed close together. Cars supposedly traveling on streets should have appropriate distance between them.

Make sure vehicles in parking lots or at loading docks have appropriate space around them. For example, trucks parked at a loading dock that obviously didn't have enough room to maneuver to the dock tend to kill the illusion.

CHAPTER SIX

Passenger terminals and stations

A signature structure in any medium-size to large city was its passenger train station or terminal. Depending upon the number of railroads serving the city, this could be a station serving a single railroad, or a union station, where multiple railroads shared trackage and a structure to serve passengers, **1**.

St. Louis Union Station was among the largest passenger terminals in the country. Its 42 stub-ended station tracks (32 of them under the 600-foot-wide arched train shed) served more than 200 trains of 17 railroads through the 1940s. *Al Rung, Trains magazine*

New York City's Grand Central Terminal is regarded as the country's premier passenger station. The Beaux-Arts style station opened in 1913, and hosted 500-plus trains per day on two levels of trains below ground level. *New York Central*

Specific definitions can get fuzzy, but a basic distinction separating an urban "terminal" from a large station is that passenger trains not only stopped, but originated or terminated at the station. The station could serve multiple railroads, multiple routes of a single railroad, and/or branch lines.

Many of the largest passenger stations were not only signature structures for a city, but for a railroad as well. Unlike most small-town stations, which were built to standard plans, large-city terminals tended to be built as one-of-a kind, grand temples to transportation. Most were built from the 1890s through the 1920s, when cities were growing, passenger trains were the primary means of travel, and long-distance train travel was looked upon with a sense of grandeur and adventure.

The largest and grandest tended to be in either large destination cities or in cities that served as gateways where Eastern and Western lines connected. Notable examples include New York City's Grand Central Terminal (New York Central), **2**—widely regarded as the grandest passenger station of them all—and Pennsylvania (Penn) Station (Pennsylvania Railroad), Boston's North and South Stations, Chicago's Union Station and Dearborn Station, Kansas City Union Station, Washington (D.C.) Union Station, St. Louis Union Station, **1**, and Denver Union Station, to name just a few. However, there were dozens more that served cities across the country.

A few large cities had (or still have) multiple large terminals—Boston and New York each with two, for example.

Chicago, however, led the way with six downtown stations through the 1960s: Union Station (serving the Burlington; Pennsylvania; Gulf, Mobile & Ohio; and Milwaukee Road); North Western Station (Chicago & North Western); Dearborn Station (Santa Fe; Rock Island; Grand Trunk Western; Chicago & Eastern Illinois; Erie; Monon; Wabash); Grand Central (Baltimore & Ohio, Soo Line, Chicago Great Western; Pere Marquette); LaSalle Street Station (New York Central; Nickel Plate Road); and Central Station (Illinois Central).

The busiest of these handled upward of 200 or more trains a day, including inter-city as well as commuter trains. They were major employers—For example, Chicago Union in the early 1940s employed nearly 1,600 people (nearly 1,000 for the station itself, plus 500 restaurant and concession people employed by Fred Harvey, plus more than 100 red caps).

Most of these grand stations continued in their intended services into the 1960s, although the decline in passenger trains and traffic from the 1950s onward meant diminished grandeur and services and shrinking of tracks and train frequency, **3**. The coming of Amtrak in 1971 meant the end for many of these terminals, with services consolidated in many cities to small stations. Although many have been demolished, some still survive today, rebuilt or remodeled and serving as transportation hubs (city or commuter) or business centers.

A large passenger terminal can be the highlight of a city scene or even the focal point of an entire layout, **4**, but even at that, some selective compression will most likely be needed. Let's take a look at the key elements of passenger terminals and see how trains were handled and scheduled, with examples from small cities as well as large.

Components and design

Passenger terminals comprise several components. The most visible was generally the main station building (headhouse), serving as the entry point for passengers. This was attached to a trainshed or other shelter protecting the station tracks, which could number in the dozens. Nearby would be a coach yard, where cars would be stored and trains assembled.

Many of these stations featured ornate architecture in various styles, **5**. Columns, arched windows and openings, stained glass, clocks and clock towers, **6**, statues, and assorted carvings were common. The building's front would face a city street, with the structure typically taking up a city block or more of real estate. Multi-story stations were common.

Signs were common, proclaiming the station name and the railroad or railroads served. These were illuminated at night with spotlights or neon, **7**, making for dramatic scenes.

A key element inside these large terminals was a waiting room or grand

The Louisville & Nashville's Montgomery, Ala., terminal had lost a few of its original six tracks by this 1974 view of an Amtrak train loading. The station and 80-foot-wide train shed were built in 1898. *Jack E. Boucher, Historic American Engineering Record*

Passenger terminals can be signature scenes on a model railroad, as here on Dave Walton's freelanced HO scale Great Midwestern. It features lower-level platform tracks running under the headhouse, with trains of Milwaukee Road, Burlington, and Illinois Central currently in the station. *Dave Rickaby*

hall, along with smaller lounges or rooms and a concourse to connect everything. Ticket windows, a baggage check/claim area, reservation desks, telephone booths, restrooms, and an information center would be prominent. Baggage rooms, baggage handling, and train supplies were often handled below the main level, with underground concourses connecting to train platforms.

Many other businesses were operated (or had space leased to them) inside large stations. Typical were newsstands, coffee shops, gift shops, restaurants, drug stores, soda fountains, hotels, cocktail lounges, cigar shops, bakeries, and beauty and barber shops. Railroads often had offices at terminals, and office space could be leased to other businesses as well. Fred Harvey (and Harvey Houses) was a familiar

The Pennsylvania Railroad built Philadelphia's 30th Street Station in 1933 to replace Broad Street Station. It remains among the country's busiest passenger stations. Shown here in the 1970s, it has six upper-level tracks for suburban services, with through tracks in a lower level parallel to the river. *Jack E. Boucher, Historic American Engineering Record*

name to travelers, operating restaurants and hotels in stations and along railroads throughout the West.

Many terminals had their own power plants, usually solid brick buildings marked with tall smokestacks.

The settings for these stations varied widely. Many large-city terminals were surrounded by tall buildings. Grand Central, for example, had its approach tracks underground—real estate was valuable enough in New York City that neighboring structures were built above the tracks. Others, including St. Louis and Dallas (photo 18 in Chapter 1), were more in the open, with all of their trackage visible.

Outside the main entrance, a taxi stand would be prominent, and taxis would often have their own loading area or lane—Chicago Union, for example, could load more than 1,000 taxis in an

The Milwaukee Road's Minneapolis Depot, built in 1899, is an example of a smaller big-city terminal. It featured a large train shed covering five stub tracks (at right) and three-story, Renaissance Revival-style head house with 100-foot-tall clock tower. *Library of Congress*

Stations typically carried signs for their owning or operating railroads, which could be dramatic at night. This is Chicago Union; Fred Harvey (sign at left) operated food and concessions at the station. *Mel Patrick*

hour during peak times. Most stations were served by streetcar lines and later city buses. Some urban terminals had parking lots or nearby ramps; others offered only limited on-street parking. Many simply opened to streets or down steps; some terminals had decorative front garden or terrace areas.

Tracks and platforms

Stations were served by trackage in three basic designs: Through, stub, and combination, **8**. At through stations, most tracks were double-ended, with tracks passing—you guessed it, through—the station. Stub-ended stations had multiple tracks that dead-ended at the station, accessible from only one end. Combination stations had a mix of through and stub-ended tracks.

Through stations were the easiest to operate, but also took up the most real estate and were difficult to work into many urban locations. They were rare among large terminals, but common among stations located at intermediate

points of railroads. Among the best-known large examples were Kansas City Union Station, **9**, Penn Station, and Dallas. Because they allowed switching from both ends and made it easy for through trains to arrive and depart with no reverse moves, through stations could handle more trains with fewer tracks compared to stub-end terminals.

Stub-ended terminals were the most cumbersome station type to operate, as all trains had to be backed in or out. However, they take up less space—critical in downtown areas—and were common for large terminals. St. Louis was the biggest example, with 42 tracks at one time; other notable stub terminals included New Orleans Union Passenger Terminal, all Chicago stations, **10**, except Union (and Union only had a couple of through tracks for switching—no trains operated in through service), and Boston (North and South).

Combination stations had one or more through tracks, providing more

switching and operational options. The best large example was Washington (D.C.) Union.

The number of tracks and specific arrangements varied widely among stations, with the busiest stub terminals having 20 or more tracks. The tracks may be on the same level as surrounding streets (as in St. Louis or Dallas), or they may be elevated (Washington) or depressed below street level (Grand Central Terminal). Large through terminals may have 10 or 12 tracks.

Platforms and tracks were covered to protect passengers from the elements. This could be done by a large shed covering the entire loading area (St. Louis is the largest example), but by the early 1900s smaller canopies that stretch along the loading tracks became standard, **11**. Typical was to have tracks paired with each canopy covering two tracks, **12**.

Platforms could be concrete, brick, or wood planks. Platforms were wide enough to allow room for passengers

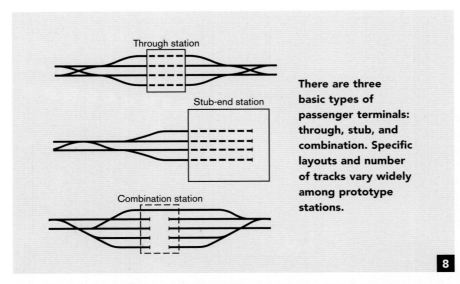

There are three basic types of passenger terminals: through, stub, and combination. Specific layouts and number of tracks vary widely among prototype stations.

8

9

Kansas City Union Station was among the country's largest through-style terminals. It opened in 1914, and the Beaux Arts-style station featured a large midway/concourse above the tracks (visible at the left behind the main building), with access to platforms via stairways. *Trains magazine collection*

as well as baggage wagons and carts. Baggage elevators were common, allowing platform access to below-ground-level service concourses.

Union stations

Many large stations are owned by single railroads, but a common arrangement in large and small cities alike is a union station, where multiple railroads share ownership of the facility with shared trackage in and around the station, **13**.

There are a number of reasons why railroads—often rivals—share a union station. Cost was a major factor—sharing a structure among two or three railroads was less expensive than each having its own building. Trackwork was also simplified, freeing more real estate for other uses.

Scheduling and connections were another factor. A union station made it easy for railroads to have their trains connect with those of other railroads, especially where railroads met end to end (and where east met west)—Chicago Union Station and St. Louis Union Station were among the largest examples.

The usual arrangement was to form a separate corporation to own the station (and accompanying trackage),

which was then in turn co-owned by the railroads involved.

Another variation was where one railroad owned the station and trackage, but leased space and services to other railroads as tenants. Examples included the Great Northern depot in Minneapolis, which also hosted trains of Northern Pacific; Burlington; Chicago Great Western; and Chicago & North Western; and Chicago's Grand Central, which was owned by the Baltimore & Ohio but also used by Soo, CGW, and Pere Marquette.

Smaller union stations were located in many cities. For example, the station at St. Joseph, Mo., **14**, into the 1950s hosted trains of the Burlington; Santa Fe; CGW; and Union Pacific. Many of these stations were quite modelable, with four to six through tracks, yet still hosted extensive operations through the 1940s. These small-city union stations were hit harder by train discontinuances than large-city stations, with many abandoned by the 1960s.

Trains and operations

How inbound and outbound trains were handled varied by location. Railroads handled their own trains at stations they owned, **15**; at shared stations, operations could be handled by individual railroads, by one railroad, or by a subsidiary terminal railroad that did all switching.

At St. Louis, for example, the Terminal Railroad Association (TRRA) owned Union Station and the related track; it was in turn owned by the railroads that operated trains at the station. Likewise in Chicago, Dearborn Station was owned and operated by the Chicago & Western Indiana, which in turn was co-owned by each of the station's railroads and handled their switching duties (except for Santa Fe, which was a non-owner tenant and switched its own trains).

Switching duties at terminals could be extensive, requiring multiple switch engines and crews. As an example, St. Louis (see the sidebar on page 86) handled more than 200 trains each day in the 1940s: That means an average of nine trains an hour—more during peak times—had to be set or pulled on one

A Monon RS-2 shoves cars down one of Dearborn Station's 10 stub-ended tracks in 1966. The big Lee Overalls sign was a landmark, just to the left of the clock tower at the station's head house. *Louis A. Marre collection*

Galesburg was an important junction station on the Burlington Route, with lines radiating to Chicago, the Twin Cities, St. Louis, Kansas City, and Denver. The five-track station had conventional canopies between pairs of tracks. *Henry J. McCord*

Dearborn's unique shed featured an open design, with a truss framework that supported narrow canopies that stretched between pairs of tracks. The platform is wood planks. Here Erie's *Lake Cities* prepares for departure in the 1950s. *Wallace W. Abbey*

Louisville Union Station, at right, hosted trains of Louisville & Nashville, Pennsylvania, and Monon. This circa 1940 view also shows, at left, the headquarters building of the L&N, along with the L&N freight house and express buildings. *Louisville & Nashville*

By large-city standards, the five-track union station at St. Joseph, Mo., was small, but it hosted 44 trains of five railroads in the 1940s. On the late afternoon of July 16, 1949, the Chicago Great Western's *Mill Cities Limited* and Burlington's motor-car *Chariton Local* are in the station. Operations at the station ceased in 1961. *Don Smith*

of the station's 42 stub-ended tracks.

These operations required coordination among railroads. An advantage is that these daily operations weren't random—they followed regular patterns, although holiday travel, special groups, and other factors could make schedule and equipment modifications necessary. Late trains and bad weather could also throw regular operations out of sequence.

Operations varied depending upon whether a train was originating, terminating, or continuing to another destination. Arriving trains generally pulled into stations using their own power, then when empty—unless the same consist of cars would be reused immediately for an outbound train— was pulled (usually by a switcher) to the nearby coach yard, where cars would be cleaned and readied for their next assignments.

A Milwaukee Road switcher sets cars on the track at right at the railroad's Minneapolis depot in July 1950. The station also hosted trains of Rock Island (center) as a Milwaukee F-M Erie Built awaits action at left. *Henry J. McCord*

Passenger cars for departing trains were generally "set"—placed on their station tracks—a couple of hours in advance of departure to allow passengers to board in advance, **15**. Sleeping-car passengers were sometimes given the option of boarding several hours in advance as a convenience, especially for trains departing in the overnight hours.

Head-end cars, including Railway Post Office cars as well as baggage and express cars of mail and express parcels, would be added to these consists shortly before departure, again by a switcher. The road power for the train would then be added, and would pull the departing train out when cleared for departure.

Through trains—those arriving at a station and continuing onward after the station stop—may perform a number of duties. Locomotives can be added, removed, or swapped (the latter common in the steam era). Head-end express and mail cars can be added and removed—this is sometimes done by the road power; other times by a switching locomotive. Passenger cars may be dropped off or picked up—this was especially common for sleeping cars. Some trains were divided or combined at intermediate stations.

Coach yards were passenger-car yards located near major passenger stations and terminals, **16**. They served as more than storage areas: Here cars were cleaned, serviced, washed, and

Two Burlington E8s lead the Great Northern *Empire Builder* out of Chicago Union Station and past the coach yards of Burlington (left) and Pennsylvania (right) in June 1951. Here is where passenger trains were assembled and cars maintained. *Wallace W. Abbey*

stocked for their next assignments. Structures supporting these yards included warehouses for commissaries (for restocking diners and lounge cars) and other supplies; laundries for taking care of sleeping-car blankets and linens, and wash racks for cleaning car exteriors.

Railroad freight yards were often nearby, along with an associated locomotive servicing terminal, where passenger road power would be brought to and from the passenger terminal.

The extensive trackwork at stations, coupled with frequent train movements, made traffic control

very important. The usual solution at most major terminals was an interlocking tower, generally located near the station's approach tracks. From the tower, operators controlled switches and signals throughout the terminal by moving levers that were interlocked with each other to ensure that conflicting routes were not set. The levers powered devices pneumatically, electrically, or a combination. If a tower wasn't used, switch tenders on the ground would be responsible for lining switches and routes.

This aerial view from 1923 looks east, with the yard throat tracks and interlocking tower at center. The trainshed is to the left. The express buildings in the foreground were demolished in 1929 and 10 new station tracks added in their place.
Clint Murphy

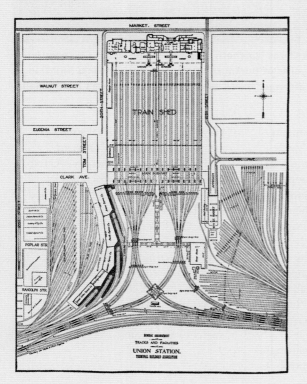

St. Louis Union Station

As an example, let's take a look at one of the country's largest terminals, St. Louis Union Station. The city was the second-largest gateway (behind Chicago) between eastern and western railroads, but unlike Chicago, which had six major passenger stations, St. Louis had a single large terminal.

Built in 1894, St. Louis Union was the country's largest passenger station at the time (and possibly the world). The Romanesque headhouse measured 81 x 601 feet, with a similar-sized "midway" concourse linking it to the massive trainshed. Its grand hall waiting room had a 65-foot vaulted ceiling, and the station had a 280-foot clock tower. The station featured a hotel and multiple restaurants and retail stores.

Initially, 11 railroads used the station; this grew to 22 at its peak, but through consolidations by the 1940s, the station served 17 railroads: Alton; Baltimore & Ohio; Chicago & Eastern Illinois; Chicago, Burlington & Quincy; Louisville & Nashville; Missouri-Kansas-Texas; Missouri Pacific; Nickel Plate Road; Gulf, Mobile & Ohio; Illinois Central; New York Central; Nickel Plate Road; Pennsylvania; St. Louis-San Francisco; St. Louis Southwestern; Southern; and Wabash.

This is the fireman's view as a Missouri Pacific train backs into the train shed in 1951. The brakes are controlled from the rear of the train for this maneuver. *Missouri Pacific*

The decorative iron fencing and gates that divided the concourse from the train shed were taken down in 1942 during a World War II scrap drive. Note the train boards, track number signs, and phone booths. *Terminal Railroad Association*

A Terminal Railroad Association switcher crosses the diamonds under the signal bridge in front of the control tower in the late 1940s. *Henry J. McCord*

In 1914 the station hosted 288 trains per day; during its busiest period of World War II it handled about 210 trains and almost 70,000 passengers daily (more than 100,000 daily passengers on peak days).

The track plan shows the station's unique arrangement. The train shed is massive: 600 feet wide, 630 feet long, with an arched roof 74 feet tall at its peak. The shed covered 32 parallel stub-ended tracks that abutted the station's midway (concourse). Each side of 16 tracks funneled down to three tracks, each set of which—in an inverted Y—branched and divided so all station tracks could all be switched from the east or west.

The express company buildings (on the left of the drawings, and in the foreground of photo at top left) were torn down in 1929, and an additional 10 station tracks were added in their place.

These diverging tracks crossed in front of the train shed at an interlocking tower, which controlled all moves within the station complex. At peak operations, eight operators controlled the plant's 315 signals and 315 switches. Extensive coach yards on either side of the approach tracks stored and sorted cars of the railroads serving the station.

All switching operations were handled by Terminal Railway Association switchers (TRRA owned the station; TRRA was in turn owned by the railroads that operated at the station). Inbound trains usually backed into place on the station tracks with their road power; cars for departing trains were set on the tracks by TRRA switchers, with power eventually added at the open end of the shed so trains pulled out forward. This kept locomotives out of (or at the far end of) the shed to minimize smoke and noise.

The station remained busy through the 1940s, but passenger traffic began a rapid decline in the 1950s, and by 1960 several tracks had been removed. On the eve of Amtrak, just a dozen trains of seven railroads used the station; that number shrunk further when Amtrak took over in 1971. Unable to justify the space, Amtrak pulled out of the station in 1978. The station has since been refurbished and serves as a retail and dining center in St. Louis.

Modeling a station such as St. Louis requires some creativity and selective compression. For example, modeling just the head house/midway and train shed to scale would take an area of 6'-10" x 9'-4" in HO scale and 3'-9" x 5'-1" in N scale—and that doesn't include any of the approach trackage or TRRA main line.

It's usually best to capture the overall flavor of a station, eliminating tracks while keeping distinctive features: For example, modeling 8 to 12 tracks instead of 32, with one or two tracks forming each leg of the distinctive wye instead of the prototype's three tracks.

CHAPTER SEVEN

Streetcars and electric railways

A Milwaukee streetcar waits for pedestrians at Third Street and Michigan in 1947. It's easy to see the appeal of streetcar modeling, with the colorful cars, period vehicles, signs, and track in brick streets. *T.H. Desnoyers; Krambles-Peterson collection*

Streetcars, operating on rails in streets and electrically powered by overhead wire, were a common sight in cities of all sizes (and even in some smaller towns) from the 1890s through the 1930s—later in some areas, **1**. Other electric railways using their own rights-of-way were developed in many areas as well.

Although not frequently modeled, electric traction (named for the electric traction motors that power the equipment) lines are an active niche segment of the hobby, and electric railroads have a definite appeal among modelers, **2**. This can mean simply adding a streetcar line to an existing layout, or basing an entire model railroad on a streetcar, interurban, or heavy electric railroad.

Prototype electric railways first appeared in the late 1800s as electricity came into wide use in American cities. Streetcars were an efficient early way to move lots of people in densely populated areas. Because a self-powered trolley or streetcar weighed less than a steam locomotive or conventional passenger car, electric railways could be built with lighter rail, tighter curves, steeper grades, and lighter bridges—making installation less expensive.

Electric lines eliminated issues with pollution from steam locomotives—critical in crowded urban areas.

Streetcars could stand idle until needed, unlike steam locomotives, which needed constant tending.

By the turn of the 20th century, streetcar lines were being built in cities across the country, and lines were also being built between towns—interurbans. Meanwhile, steam railroads were beginning to string overhead wire and use heavy electric locomotives in high-density areas and mountainous regions.

Streetcars

Streetcars first operated as horse-drawn carriages ("horsecars"), with the first U.S. line operating in 1832 in New York City, **3**. These cars could carry more passengers with less resistance than a conventional horsewagon on the street, and the steel wheels and rails offered a smoother ride. More than 400 street railways were in service in the U.S. using horsecars by the 1880s.

The first successful electric street railway using overhead power was installed in Richmond, Va., in 1888,

and electric systems were soon being installed in other cities. Electric streetcars could move faster and were efficient—horses were labor-intensive to keep.

Streetcar lines followed the same basic construction as steam railroads, but their lightweight single cars didn't require support like track that had to handle steam locomotives and long strings of heavy freight cars. As Chapter 2 noted, this meant lighter rail, steeper grades, tighter curves, and sharper turnout angles.

City lines kept to one-way operation whenever possible. This meant double-track was common, with a track in each street lane, so cars could follow the direction of vehicle traffic. At the end of lines, this track typically looped for the return trip. Most cars were bi-directional, with controls at each end and two trolley poles. Changing directions was a matter of lowering one pole, going to the other end of the car, and raising the trailing pole.

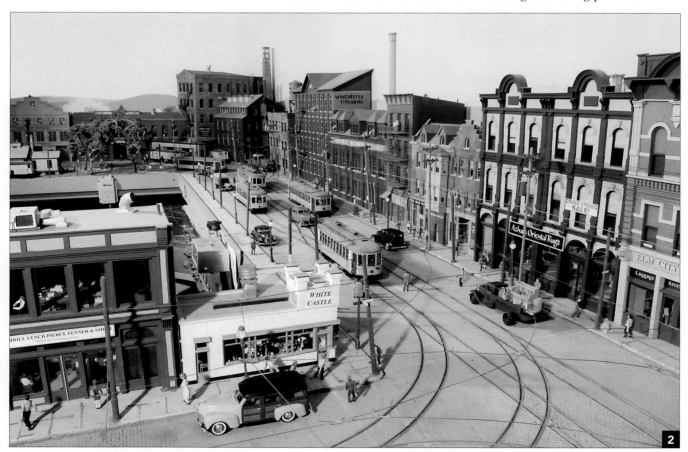

Les Lewis models the Connecticut Company on his basement-size O scale layout. The structures in this city, based on New Haven, are scratchbuilt. *Fred M. Dole*

A horse-drawn streetcar trundles down Eighth Avenue in New York City in the 1890s. Some horse-drawn cars lasted in the city until 1917. *Library of Congress*

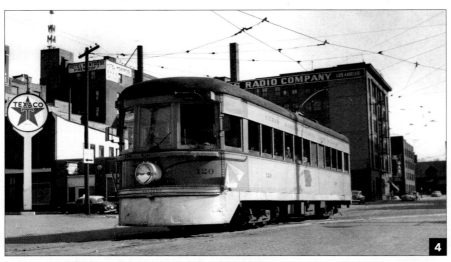

A Cedar Rapids & Iowa City interurban car rolls down a street in Cedar Rapids, Iowa, prior to the line's passenger-train discontinuance in 1953. The line continues today as a freight-only operator with diesel locomotives.

Trains magazine collection

Large cities with multiple routes had complex trackwork. Large central terminals were common in downtown areas to coordinate passenger transfers.

The rise in popularity of the automobile from the 1920s onward doomed streetcar lines, and their number began to drop—especially in smaller cities and towns—and routes on larger systems were cut back. The Depression accelerated the process, with many street systems going out of business by World War II. Some big-city lines survived through the 1940s, but most were gone by the 1950s.

Interurbans

Interurban lines followed the basic construction and design principles of streetcar lines, but connected cities and towns using a combination of private right-of-way and city streets, **4**. Typical interurban practice was to resume street running upon entering a town, either on its own track or that of the city's streetcar system (some were owned and operated by the same company).

Many interurban lines paralleled steam railroads, but swung into town as they approached. Interurban lines were usually built to heavier standards than streetcar lines (with an eye toward carrying freight cars or additional trailer cars, as opposed to just single self-contained cars), but not as heavy as standard railroads. For interurbans, 70-pound rail was usually sufficient; this was heavier than most streetcar rail

but lighter than the 90- to 110-pound rail used on most steam main lines of the era. Ballast was rare on all but the busiest lines, and sidings were short.

Interurban cars were generally larger, longer, and heavier than streetcars. This could create clearance problems along some city streetcar lines, where interurbans—especially when pulling freight cars—were sometimes limited to using certain tracks.

Interurbans became especially popular from around 1900 through the 1920s, and were most common in the Midwest and plains states. However, the largest interurban operation was based in Los Angeles: Pacific Electric, **5**. This system, which emerged in the 1890s, eventually operated more than 1,000 miles of line, extending south past Long Beach to Balboa and westward through San Bernardino to Redlands. It carried freight as well as passengers.

Other well-known interurbans included the Chicago North Shore & Milwaukee; Chicago South Shore & South Bend; Fort Dodge, Des Moines & Southern; Illinois Terminal; Cedar Rapids & Iowa City; and Detroit United Railway.

Interurbans weren't just slow-traffic lines. Some were maintained to high standards and hosted fast trains. The North Shore's Electroliners, for example, could travel at 90 mph on the line's private right-of-way between Chicago and Milwaukee, **6**. The line's high-speed, frequent service allowed it to operate into the 1960s.

Many interurban lines had passenger service only, but some also hauled freight cars as well—typical of those that remained in service the longest. Many, even passenger lines, did significant business in express and less-than-carload, or LCL, freight. Short consists were common, with a single car or a passenger trailer or car or two; for freight, a few cars at a time, **7** (and **2-1**). Small steeple-cab locomotives were common on interurban freight lines.

Stations could be stand-alone buildings, but they were often located in storefront buildings in the center of a city, often on its main street with loading and unloading in the middle of the street, **8**. Some interurban and streetcar lines had significant-sized passenger terminals in larger cities.

As with streetcars, interurbans were impacted heavily by the growth of the automobile and improving highways. Most were abandoned by the early 1930s; some that handled higher levels of traffic (or freight service) lasted longer. A few were upgraded to steam standards and continued operating, with some becoming diesel-powered lines (Illinois Terminal [photo 14 in Chapter 4] and FDD&S were among the best known).

Heavy electric lines

The early 1900s saw many steam railroads ponder electrification, both as a more-efficient system and as a way to limit pollution from steam locomotives in urban areas and tunnels. What distinguishes a heavy electric line from a streetcar or interurban is that heavy electric lines carry the same traffic as a standard steam railroad, with powerful locomotives carrying full trains of passenger and freight cars on track built to conventional railroad standards, **9**.

These lines served many major metropolitan areas. The best-known are the Pennsylvania Railroad and New Haven lines that served what became the Northeast Corridor, running from Boston down through New York and Philadelphia to Washington, D.C. This line hosts some of the highest-density traffic in the country, and is still in service by Amtrak.

Passenger traffic in and out of New York's Penn Station, **10**, and Grand Central Terminal were handled by electric locomotives because of the amount of below-ground trackage in and around the stations. Cleveland Union Terminal also had electric lines at and near its station.

Heavy electric locomotives are quite powerful, with horsepower ratings from 5,000 to 7,000. General Electric and Westinghouse were the primary early builders. These locomotives use pantographs as opposed to the trolley poles of streetcars and most interurbans.

Because of the busy areas they

Pacific Electric Los Angeles-bound car no. 1101, built by Standard Steel Car in 1924, rolls in the late 1940s. Pacific Electric was the largest interurban system in the U.S., operating more than 1,000 route-miles over a combination of private right-of-way and street running. *D.K. Hedgpeon*

A North Shore Line Electroliner rolls southbound on Milwaukee's South Fifth Street just north of Mitchell on June 12, 1959. The Electroliners could do 90 mph once leaving street track for private right of way south of the city. *Fred W. Schneider*

served, trackwork and overhead wire installations are very impressive for heavy electrics, **10**, especially in yards and passenger terminals. It can be a major drawing point for modelers, **11**.

Overhead wire

Streetcars and interurbans draw their electricity from an overhead wire that runs centered above the track. The

rails and ground serve as the common return path for the circuit. A trolley pole on a pivoting base extends upward from the streetcar roof, with a grooved wheel at the top that follows the wire. (Sliding shoes became more popular in the early 1900s, and provided better contact.) Poles were usually 12 to 14 feet long and were spring-loaded to maintain solid wire contact (look at

Interurban Yakima Valley Transportation survived as an electric freight operation until 1985. Here steeplecab locomotive no. 298 (built by GE in 1922) pulls three reefers on street trackage in Yakima, Wash., in 1974. *Trains magazine collection*

Illinois Terminal train 83 (car no. 302) makes a station stop in the street at Staunton, Ill., in January 1956. The IT would abandon interurban passenger service later that year, but continue as a diesel-powered freight railroad. *John C. Illman*

A "Clocker," essentially a long-distance commuter train, passes New Rochelle Junction, N.Y., en route from New York City to Boston. The New Haven's 11,000-volt, 25-hertz, single-phase AC catenary is an impressive sight. *J.J. Farwell*

the photos and you'll see they're bowed slightly from this when in contact with the wire).

The system worked well, but the pole would occasionally slip off the wire (especially on curves or along lines with poor trackwork) to the consternation of the operator. He would have to go back and reset the pole with a rope hanging down from the pole. Sparks were common, and watching a streetcar at night could provide a significant light show.

Most cars were outfitted for two-way operation, with a pole on each end of the car. The rear pole would be extended to contact the wire, while the forward pole would be latched down to the car roof.

Heavy electric lines (and some interurbans) use pantographs, spring-loaded sliders that extend upward to contact the wire. They are more reliable than trolley shoes.

The appearance of overhead wire is complex and has considerable appeal to modelers—it's impressive to see in person or in photographs on both prototypes and models alike. The specific construction and design varied among owners, depending upon the location of track (private right-of-way or street), power used (600-volt, 1,200-volt, or higher), and speeds involved.

The contact wire (or trolley wire) is suspended above the track on a system of brackets held by poles. The contact wire is at least 18 feet above rail-height level (and no higher than 21 feet). Hangers grip the contact wire using clamps, so that the bottom surface of the wire is clear for the trolley wheel, shoe, or pantograph.

Span wires are located crosswise between poles (for example, on opposite sides of a street) to hold the contact wire. Pull-off wires are used on curves, **12**, to keep the wire aligned above the track.

Line poles for most streetcar lines were wood, reinforced with guy wires where needed. More substantial installations used reinforced concrete posts. In street installations, the poles may also be used to carry electricity and communication lines—especially in the cities where the streetcar line was owned by the electric company. On these, a crossarm for communication wires would be above the feeder wire, with electric lines on the tallest crossarm at the top of the pole.

For heavy electric operations (and some interurbans), a messenger wire ran directly above the contact wire. The messenger held the contact wire through a series of downward wires (hangers). This allows the messenger wire to sag between poles while keeping the contact wire level (visible in New Haven and PRR photos).

Feeder wires were the wires that supplied power to the contact wire. The feeder or feeders were on insulators, typically on a crossarm on the pole above the bracket.

Bigger installations on private right-of-way typically used truss-style bridges to span track and support the wires. On these, the primary messenger wire would be carried above the bridge on insulators, with a secondary messenger below the bridge arms, then the contact wire on hangers below the secondary messenger.

On railroads using pantographs, the contact wire doesn't follow a straight line down the middle of the track. Instead it zig-zags slightly from side to side (about 6" each side of center) to even the wear on the pan contacts.

Third-rail power

An alternative to the often-complex overhead wire was using an electrified third rail to the outside of the running rails, **4-24**. A retractable sliding plate ("shoe") mounted on the interurban car's or locomotive's truck frame contacted the rail to draw power. Third-rail was easier to install and maintain and didn't have overhead clearance issues, so it became common in and around passenger terminals, in subways, and along many other routes. Many streetcars, interurbans, and electric locomotives were equipped with both overhead and third-rail pickup, allowing them to switch as needed.

The third rail itself could be located on either side of the track, minimizing interference from turnouts and other obstacles. Where the third

A New Haven rectifier electric pauses at the west end of New York's Pennsylvania Station in 1960. *Jim Shaughnessy*

A New York, New Haven & Hartford EP-5 pulls an eastbound passenger train around Jenkins Curve on Richard Abramson's HO scale New Haven layout. The distinctive New Haven catenary bridges are available from Model Memories. *Richard Abramson*

Pull-off wires keep the contact wire aligned over curves. You can also see how the hangers clamp to the contact wire. This is the tunnel at Maverick Square in Boston in 1906. *Library of Congress*

Streetcar lines often featured tight curves and interesting trackwork, like this switch in Portland, Ore., where the points sent the diverging route one way before the curve went another to make a sharper corner. *Linn H. Westcott*

Single-point turnouts (the point at left) were often used on streetcar lines. This is on Yakima Valley Transportation at Yakima, Wash. *Jigger Schmidt, Historic American Engineering Record*

rail is interrupted, the rail ends taper downward to make engaging the rail smoother. Many grade crossings result in a dead spot—trains rely on multiple pickup points for power, so that at least one of multiple shoes are engaged.

In most areas the powered rail is covered by an inverted-L-shaped wood guard that covers the top and outside of the rail, protecting people and animals from accidentally contacting the rail. Fenced right-of-way and restricted access is used whenever practical.

Street trackage

Chapter 2 covered street construction, modeling, and trackage in streets. Remember that streetcar trackage could have sharper curves, sharper turnouts, steeper hills, and more funky trackwork, **13**, than conventional railroad track in streets.

Streetcar track used a variety of cast components with girder rail. Turnouts often had just a single point, **14**. Streetcar lines also often used spring

Pennsylvania RR GG1 electric no. 4814 leads a train into Penn Station in New York in the mid-1940s. The train is emerging from the Manhattan end of the Hudson River tunnel. *Frank Clodfelter*

switches: These are set to direct traffic to a single route, but with points that are sprung to allow oncoming traffic from either route to pass through.

Modeling

Traction modeling is a specialized, niche part of the hobby. Some modelers choose to include streetcars as part of a larger layout; others have made streetcars, interurbans, or heavy electrics the focal point of an entire model railroad.

Another very viable option is to include a stretch of "dummy" streetcar track on your layout, with a length of track and overhead wire with a stationary (non-operating) car or two. This can be a manageable modeling project, since the track and wire are just scenery.

Advantages to modeling streetcar lines is that the small equipment and tight curves enable packing a lot of action into a small area. If urban modeling is your primary interest, it's worth a look.

The main challenge of traction modeling is the overhead wire. As with the prototype, it takes careful initial installation and regular maintenance to keep it operating smoothly. Most traction layouts are wired so that the track is one polarity while the overhead line is the other. Another option is wiring track like a conventional layout, with the overhead wire strictly for decoration.

The coming of Digital Command Control (DCC) and the availability of smooth-operating motors has been a boon to streetcar modeling, especially for modelers who want to operate busy systems with lots of cars in operation. Automated (or partially automated) operation is another realistic possibility.

Books on modeling include *Traction Guidebook for Model Railroaders* (Kalmbach, 1974), and *Traction Planbook, Second Edition*, by Harold H. Carstens (Carstens Publishing, 1968). Although both are out of print, you can still find copies (check eBay and abebooks.com), and although both are

dated they include good information if you want to model overhead wire. Many magazine articles have also been published.

Traction components have been offered by several manufacturers. The Orr line of HO track is now available from CustomTraxx (www.customtraxx. com), which is also a great site to see other products currently available. Ready-to-run HO scale streetcars have been offered by Bowser, which also has a line of mechanisms; Bachmann; and Con-Cor. Other manufacturers have included Bronze Key, Clouser, and Suydam; models and components often show up on eBay.

The East Penn Traction Club is one of the oldest groups focusing on traction modeling, and its website is a good source of information (eastpenn.org). Another is the Illinois Traction Society (www.illinoistractionsociety.org).

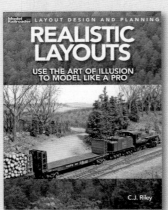
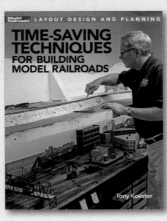
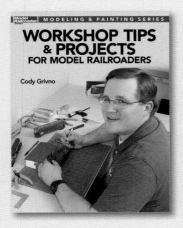
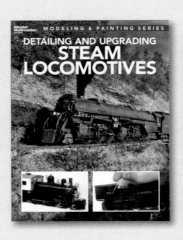